The All Color Book of

Bible Stories

Retold by Patricia J. Hunt
Illustrated by Giovanni Caselli

octopus

The Old Testament

First published in 1978 by
Octopus Books Limited,
59 Grosvenor Street,
London W1.

© 1978 Hennerwood Publications Limited
ISBN 0 7064 0836 5

Printed in Great Britain by
Jarrold & Sons Limited

The New Testament

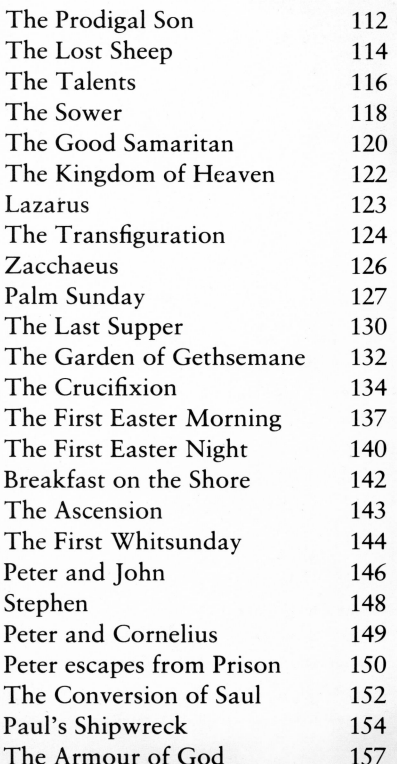

The Creation

IN the very beginning, when there was no shape to the world and everywhere was darkness, there was God. There has never been a time when he did not exist.

Then God said, 'Let there be light' and there was light. God was pleased with what he saw, and he divided the light from the dark. He called the light day and the dark he called night.

The next day God made the sky, like a great dome over the earth.

On the third day God made dry land, which he called earth. He also made the waters, which he called seas. On the earth he put grass and seeds and trees which grew fruit.

On the fourth day God made light to mark the seasons and the days and the years. He made the greater light, called the sun, to rule the day, and the lesser light, called the moon, to shine at night. He also made the stars. The world God made was very beautiful.

There were not yet any living creatures in the world. So on the fifth day God made great whales and sea-monsters and all kinds of smaller fish to live in the deep blue waters. He filled the sky with beautiful birds to fly over the green earth.

The seas and skies teemed with life, and God was pleased with his work.

On the sixth day God made all kinds of animals, some tiny and some enormous, to move about on the land. Everything was perfect and beautifully made.

However there was no one to till the ground or to look

after the growing plants and trees. There was no one to take care of the fish and the birds and the animals. So finally, on the sixth day, God said, 'Now I will make man, in my likeness. This man will take care of all the living things I have made that move in the sky and sea and on land.'

God was pleased with his work, and on the next day, the seventh, he rested. He blessed the seventh day and made it holy, and ever since one day in seven has been a day for resting from work.

After God had made man, he planted a beautiful garden in a place called Eden. There were all sorts of lovely trees in this garden, on which grew the choicest fruits. There were also two special trees – one called the Tree of Life and the other called the Tree of the Knowledge of Good and Evil.

A river flowed out of Eden to water the garden, and God put the man he had made into the garden to look after it. He named the man Adam and he meant him to be very happy.

'You may eat the fruits of any of the trees in the garden,' God said to Adam, 'except the Tree of the Knowledge of Good and Evil. You must not eat that, for if you do, you will die.'

Then God decided that Adam should have a companion. While Adam was asleep, God made a woman to share his life and the garden with him. The woman became Adam's wife and Adam named her Eve. They lived happily together, working in God's beautiful garden.

Adam and Eve

LIVING in the Garden of Eden was a serpent who was more cunning than any of the other creatures which God had made.

One day, he slithered up to Eve and said, 'Did God tell you not to eat the fruit of the trees in the garden?'

'No,' said Eve, 'we may eat any we like, except the fruit that grows on the Tree of the Knowledge of Good and Evil. We must not eat that one or we shall die.'

The crafty serpent hissed, 'You won't really die, you know. God only said that to stop you from knowing all about good and evil because then you would be as great as he is.'

Eve looked at the tree. The fruit certainly looked tempting, and she wanted to try it. So she picked one of the fruits, took a bite, and then gave it to Adam who had some too.

All at once, they both felt very ashamed of what they had done. They knew now what it was to do wrong. They had chosen their own way and not God's.

That evening, they heard God walking in the garden. Adam and Eve tried to hide among the trees, for they knew they had disobeyed him and they were ashamed of themselves.

'Adam,' called God, 'where are you?'

'I heard you coming,' Adam replied, 'and I was afraid, so I hid myself.'

'Have you eaten the fruit of the tree I told you not to touch?' asked God. He knew that this was the only thing that could make them unhappy and afraid.

'Eve gave me the fruit and I ate it,' said Adam miserably.

Eve hung her head in shame and said, 'The serpent tricked me into it.'

God was very sad and displeased. He turned to the serpent and said, 'Because you have done this, you will always have to crawl along in the dust of the earth for the rest of your life.'

God decided that Adam and Eve could no longer be trusted and must not be allowed to remain in the garden. He told them they would have to leave it and work in the outside world. Life could no longer be as happy as God had intended.

Sadly Adam and Eve left the Garden of Eden.

Cain and Abel

ADAM and Eve had two sons called Cain and Abel. Cain became a farmer and Abel became a shepherd. One day they both made an offering to God. Cain brought a gift of his very best crops, while Abel brought his fattest lambs.

God was pleased with Abel's offering, which was given in the right spirit of faith, but he did not find Cain's gift acceptable. This made Cain very angry, for he was jealous of Abel.

'Why are you so angry?' God asked him. 'If you give cheerfully and willingly, your gift will also be acceptable. But if you don't give in the right way, you are likely to do evil.'

Cain did not answer. He just let his anger grow stronger inside him, until one day he quarrelled with Abel when they were out in the fields, and killed him.

Afterwards God asked him, 'Where is your brother Abel?'

Cain was frightened and made things worse by saying, 'I don't know. Am I supposed to know where he is all the time?'

God knows everything and he said, 'Because you have killed your brother, you must leave here and wander about the world for the rest of your life.'

Cain was frightened, thinking that as he wandered someone would try to kill him. However, God would not let this happen. He put a special mark on Cain as a warning to others not to kill him.

Noah's Ark

BANG! Bang! Bang, went the hammers, as old Noah worked hard at building his boat. When finished, there would be three decks inside it – a bottom, a middle and an upper deck – and there would be a roof, a door and windows. It would be 133 metres long, 22 metres wide and 13 metres high. It was all to be made of a special wood called gopher wood.

Helping Noah were his three sons, Shem, Ham and Japheth.

'What are you doing, Noah?' the neighbours asked.

'God has told me to build a boat – an ark,' said Noah.

'But why?' asked the neighbours. 'There isn't enough water here to sail a boat of that size.'

'God says there is a great flood coming,' replied Noah, 'and it will destroy everyone on the earth because they have been so wicked and thought only about themselves.'

'Nonsense!' laughed the neighbours.

'God said I was to build this ark,' went on Noah, 'and to take my family and two of every kind of animal and bird into it and there we shall be safe.'

'Fancy believing that!' scoffed the people. 'We don't care about what God says, and we don't believe in him either. You will look silly with a big boat like that on dry land!'

Noah refused to be put off. He tried to make them understand that it was right to obey God and to live by his laws, but they just would not listen. So he and his sons went on sawing and hammering at the boat because that was what God had told them to do.

Meanwhile Noah's wife and the sons' wives began to prepare food and to collect together all the clothes the family would need when they went to live in the ark.

When the building of the ark was finished, Noah covered it with tar, as God had directed, to make quite sure that it was thoroughly waterproof.

Then, when at last the ark was quite ready, Noah and his family began to round up two of every kind of animal and bird and guide them into the ark. There were two lions, two tigers, two giraffes, two elephants, two mice, two ravens, two doves – two of all living creatures, even tiny spiders and ladybirds.

Last of all Noah and his wife, and his sons and their wives, went in and Noah shut the door.

A week went by. Then it started to pour with rain, and it rained in torrents, without stopping, for forty days and forty nights.

The water rose higher and higher and the ark rocked as it began to float. Soon all the trees and buildings were covered and when Noah looked out of the windows, he could see nothing but water. Only the people and the animals in the ark were still alive.

The water covered the earth for a hundred and fifty days, and the ark floated along on the top. Then the winds started to blow and the water began to go down, and the ark came to rest on a mountain called Mount Ararat.

One day Noah said, 'I will send out a dove to see if there is any dry land,' but the dove came back because she could find nowhere to land.

Noah waited a week and then he sent out the dove again. This time she came back with an olive leaf in her beak.

'The waters must have gone down low enough for the trees to be appearing,' said Noah.

Another week passed, and Noah sent out the dove a third time. She did not return and Noah knew she must have found a new home among the trees.

About four weeks later Noah opened the door of the ark. The water had all gone and the earth was dry. Then God said, 'Now you may leave the ark.'

Noah came out with his family and all the living creatures whom God had kept safely in the ark during the flood.

The first thing Noah did was to collect some stones and to build an altar where he could thank God for keeping them all safe.

Then God made a promise to Noah. 'As long as earth remains,' he said, 'there will always be springtime and harvest, cold and heat, summer and winter, day and night. There will never be another flood like this one. As a sign of my promise, I will place a rainbow in the sky.'

The Tower of Babel

LONG after the days of Noah and the flood, the people on earth were like one enormous family, all speaking the same language.

They began to travel eastwards until they reached a plain in the land of Shinar. It was near the Persian Gulf and not far from the great rivers Tigris and Euphrates. Here they settled down and made their plans.

They felt very important and wanted to make a great name for themselves which would be remembered for ever.

They had also begun to find out how to use building materials and they were becoming very clever but they were forgetting about God. He no longer seemed important to them.

'Let us make bricks,' they said, 'and build ourselves a city with a huge tower – so high that its top reaches right into the heavens. This will keep us together and it will be for ever a splendid memorial to us.'

They thought that the tower, which would look very magnificent, would make them secure against enemy invaders. How proud they felt as they began work!

Everyone helped and soon the tower began to grow quite high. God saw what they were doing and he knew that it was wrong. He knew that they had left him out of their lives, thinking only of how clever they were. He knew that they could not reach heaven by building a tower.

God wanted the best for his children and he could see that the way they were behaving would lead them into evil ways. Already there was a great deal of quarrelling and jealousy. They were becoming very arrogant and proud.

'I will scatter the people all over the earth,' God said, 'and I will change their ways of speaking, so that they can no longer understand each other.'

So that is what he did. The people stopped building their tower. They left the city and moved off in different directions, forming their own separate settlements and speaking different languages.

Because of this, the city was called Babel, which meant confusion in Hebrew.

Abraham and Sarah

ABRAHAM lived in the land of Canaan with his wife Sarah. God had given this land to him and his descendants.

One hot afternoon Abraham was sitting outside his tent, when he saw three strangers coming towards him. He ran to make them welcome. Then he and Sarah prepared a large meal and he brought it out to the visitors.

The visitors asked, 'Where is Sarah your wife?'

'She is in the tent,' replied Abraham.

Then one of the visitors said, 'In the spring she will have a son.'

Now Sarah was just inside the tent door and she heard what the stranger said. 'A son, after all these years?' she thought. 'Abraham and I are much too old to have children.' She laughed at the very idea.

God knew what Sarah was thinking, and he said to Abraham, 'Why did Sarah laugh? Is there anything which is too hard for the Lord?'

Abraham then knew that if God had planned it, Sarah would indeed have a son.

When the visitors rose to go, Abraham walked with them part of the way, for he now realized who they were. He knew he had been entertaining messengers from God.

God's promise came true. Abraham and Sarah had a baby son. They called him Isaac, for God had said that this was to be his name.

Abraham's Sacrifice

ABRAHAM'S son, Isaac, grew up to be a fine boy.
Abraham and Sarah loved him so much that one day
God decided to test Abraham's faith.

'Abraham, take your son, your only son Isaac, whom you
love so much, and go to the mountain of Moriah to a place
which I will show you. I want you to give me your son as a
sacrifice.'

Abraham could scarcely believe he had heard correctly.
Yet he knew God's will must be obeyed. He called Isaac and
told him that they were going into the mountains early the
next morning. Isaac helped him to collect wood for the fire
and to load their donkey. Then with Isaac and two servants,
he set off for the place God had told him.

After three days' journey they came to the mountain, and
Abraham told the servants to wait with the donkey while he
and Isaac went on to worship. Isaac carried wood for the
fire, while Abraham took a knife.

'Father,' said Isaac, 'we have the wood and the knife, but
where is the lamb which we are to offer to God for a sacrifice?'

'God will see to that,' said Abraham with a heavy heart.

They walked on together and when they reached the top,
Abraham began to build an altar. He put the wood on it
ready for the fire, and then bound Isaac and laid him on the
wood. Then he took the knife and was just about to sacrifice
Isaac when an angel of the Lord called to him from heaven.

'Abraham! Abraham! Do not hurt the boy – for now I
know that you really trust God, seeing that you were ready
to give him your only son.'

How relieved Abraham felt! Then, looking up, he saw a
ram which was caught by its horns in a nearby bush. Abraham
released his son and offered the ram to God instead. Father
and son were very happy as they went home together.

Jacob and Esau

ISAAC and his wife Rebecca had twin sons. The elder was called Esau and the younger was Jacob. As the elder, Esau would become head of the family. Isaac loved Esau best, while Jacob was Rebecca's favourite.

When Isaac was very old he could hardly see and found it difficult to tell Esau from Jacob.

One day he called Esau to him. 'Take your bow and arrows,' he said, 'and go out hunting. Bring me my favourite meat to eat and then I will give you my blessing before I die.'

Rebecca overheard this and she wanted Jacob to have Isaac's blessing. So she told Jacob to fetch two young goats from the flock.

'If you take the meat to him,' she said, 'he will bless *you* instead of Esau.'

'But Mother,' said Jacob, 'Esau's hands are hairy and mine are smooth, so even though Father can't see, he'll know as soon as he touches me that I'm not Esau.'

However, Rebecca had a plan. She dressed Jacob in Esau's clothes, and on his smooth hands and neck she put the hairy skins of the goats.

'Who are you?' asked Isaac, peering at Jacob as he came in.

'I am Esau, your elder son,' said Jacob. 'I have done as you asked. Now, sit up and eat this food and then give me your blessing.'

'Come nearer,' said Isaac, 'so that I can really feel that you are Esau.'

Jacob went closer and his father touched him. Then he said in a puzzled tone, 'The voice sounds like Jacob, but the hands feel like Esau. Are you really my son Esau?'

Jacob answered, 'Yes, I am.'

'Come near and kiss me,' said Isaac, and Jacob did so. Isaac could smell the fields on Esau's clothes, and now he felt sure that this really was his son Esau. He ate the food and then gave Jacob the blessing which should have been Esau's.

Jacob had scarcely left his father when Esau came back.

'Sit up and eat this, father, and then you can bless me,' said the real Esau.

'But who are you?' asked the bewildered Isaac.

'I'm your elder son, Esau.'

Isaac began to tremble. 'Your brother must have tricked me and he had the blessing which should have been yours.'

Esau hated Jacob and determined that, after their father's death, he would kill him if he could. Rebecca sent Jacob to stay with his uncle until Esau had conquered his anger.

Jacob's Dream

JACOB set off on the long journey to Haran where his Uncle Laban lived. Each evening when the sun set, he would stop and rest for the night. One night something strange happened to him.

He had placed a stone to use as a pillow and lay down to sleep, for he was very tired. As he slept, he had a wonderful dream. He saw a ladder, reaching from the earth right up into heaven. There were angels of God going up and down the ladder, and God himself stood at the very top.

God said to him, 'I am the God of Abraham and the God of Isaac. The land on which you are resting will be for you and your children. You will have many descendants, and they will spread to the north, south, east and west. The nations of the earth will be blessed through you and your descendants. I shall comfort you and take care of you always.'

Jacob awoke, feeling frightened. 'The Lord is in this place and I did not know!' he said. 'How holy it is!'

Then he took the stone he had used as a pillow and stood it upright. He poured oil on it, to mark the spot where he had had the dream and he named the place Bethel, which means house of God. Next he made a vow that he would always be true to God. 'Of all that he gives me,' Jacob declared, 'I will give one tenth back to him.'

24

Jacob and Rachel

AFTER many days of travelling, Jacob came near Haran. Some shepherds were waiting by a well with their sheep. Jacob asked them if they knew his Uncle Laban.

'Yes,' they replied, 'and look, here is his daughter, Rachel, coming with his sheep.'

Jacob moved the cover from the well and gave water to Rachel's sheep. He kissed her and told her he was her cousin. Rachel ran home to tell her father the news.

When Laban heard this, he took Jacob into his home and Jacob worked for him. There he came to know not only Rachel, but also her elder sister Leah.

'You shouldn't work for nothing, just because you are my relation,' said Laban. 'What shall I pay you?'

Now Jacob loved Rachel, who was very beautiful, and he said, 'I will work for you for seven years if you give me Rachel for my wife.'

Laban agreed, and Jacob worked the seven years. At the end of that time, Jacob said, 'Now give me Rachel for my wife, for the seven years are completed.'

Laban planned a great wedding party, and in the evening he took his daughter to give to Jacob. But the daughter he brought was Leah and not Rachel, and in the darkness Jacob did not know and married her. In the morning, when he found out, he was furious.

'In our country,' said Laban, 'the elder daughter comes before the younger. It would be wrong for Rachel to be married first. But if you will work for me another seven years, then Rachel will be yours.'

It was the custom in those days for men to have more than one wife, so Jacob agreed and Rachel finally became his second wife.

Joseph and his Brothers

JACOB already had ten sons when Joseph was born. Jacob loved Joseph best of all and this made the other brothers jealous. They hated Joseph even more when Jacob gave him a beautiful coat of many colours.

By the time Joseph was seventeen, he was helping his brothers to look after his father's sheep in the fields.

One night he had a dream, and the next day he told it to his brothers.

'Listen to this,' he said. 'I dreamt we were all out in the fields binding sheaves of corn. Suddenly, my sheaf stood straight up, and all your sheaves gathered round and bowed to it.'

This made the brothers very angry, for in those days dreams were often looked upon as a sign of what was to happen in the future.

'Does that mean you are going to reign over us?' they asked scornfully, and they hated him all the more.

Then Joseph had another dream, and he told that to his brothers and also to his father.

'This time,' he said, 'the sun and the moon and eleven stars all bowed before me.'

Jacob was not pleased and he said, 'Do you mean that your mother and I and all your brothers are going to bow down to you?' In spite of his angry words, Jacob wondered what it all meant, but the brothers were furious.

Some time later the brothers had gone to Shechem, a good distance away, to find pasture for their sheep. Joseph had stayed behind and Jacob said to him, 'Go and see if your brothers and the sheep are all right, and then come back and tell me.'

Joseph obeyed and set off to find them. When his brothers saw him coming, they began to plan how they could get rid of him.

'Here comes the dreamer!' they scoffed. 'Let's kill him and leave him in a pit – and we'll tell father that a wild animal caught him.'

When Joseph arrived, the brothers seized him and dragged off his beautiful coat. Instead of killing him, they decided to throw him into a deep pit. Then they sat down to have their meal.

Suddenly, they looked up as they heard camels approaching. The camels were ridden by traders on their way to Egypt.

'I know!' said one of the brothers, 'Let's sell Joseph to these men. Then we won't feel guilty about leaving him to die.'

The others agreed. They lifted Joseph out of the pit and sold him to the traders for twenty pieces of silver.

Then the brothers took Joseph's coat and dipped it in goat's blood and took it home to show Jacob.

'We found this,' they said, 'but we aren't sure whether it's Joseph's.'

Jacob knew immediately that it was the coat he had given to Joseph.

'It is my son's coat!' he cried. 'A wild animal must have caught him and torn him to pieces!'

Jacob was very sad, and mourned for Joseph so much that no one could comfort him.

Joseph in Prison

WHEN the traders arrived in Egypt they sold Joseph to Potiphar, who was captain of Pharaoh's bodyguard. (Pharaoh was the title used for the kings of Egypt.)

Potiphar took Joseph to be a servant in his house. Although he felt lonely at first, Joseph worked well and remembered that God was with him. Potiphar noticed this and was so pleased with Joseph's work, that he put him in charge of the household.

All went well until Potiphar's wife began to tell lies about Joseph. She told her husband that Joseph was behaving badly towards her, which was not true. Potiphar believed his wife and had Joseph put in prison.

God was still with him, and Joseph behaved so well that the chief jailer put him in charge of all the other prisoners.

Not long afterwards, two new prisoners arrived. They were Pharaoh's butler and his chief baker who had both offended Pharaoh in some way.

One morning Joseph went to their cell and found them looking very miserable.

'What's the matter with you two?' he asked.

'We both had strange dreams last night,' they said, 'and no one can tell us what they mean.'

'For that you need God's help,' said Joseph. 'Tell me your dreams as God may help me interpret them.'

So the butler said, 'I saw a vine with three branches that began to bud and blossom and produce ripe grapes. Pharaoh's cup was in my hand and I squeezed the grape juice into the cup and gave it to Pharaoh to drink.'

'I know what that means,' said Joseph. 'The three branches mean three days, and in three days Pharaoh will take you out of prison and you will be back in your job serving him and giving him wine as you have always done.'

This made the butler very happy, and Joseph said to him, 'When you get back, remember me and ask Pharaoh to let me out, for I have done nothing to deserve being in jail.'

When the chief baker heard how well Joseph had explained the butler's dream, he told his dream.

'There were three baskets of pastries on my head,' he said. 'In the top basket were all kinds of good things for Pharaoh to eat, but the birds flew down and ate them.'

'That means that the three baskets are three days,' said Joseph, 'and in three days' time Pharaoh will come and will take your life.'

The chief baker was very unhappy when he heard this.

Three days later it was Pharaoh's birthday, and he gave a party for all his officials and staff. He sent for his butler and his chief baker, and they were brought to him from the prison.

Then, just as Joseph had said, Pharaoh gave the butler his old job back and he sentenced the chief baker to death.

The butler went back to his work and forgot all about asking Pharaoh to free Joseph from prison. Joseph had to stay in jail in Egypt.

29

Pharaoh's Dream

JOSEPH had been in prison for two years. One night Pharaoh had two dreams which worried him very much. In the morning he sent for his magicians and wise men and told them about the dreams. No one could tell him what they meant.

Suddenly the butler remembered his own dream of two years before. He went to Pharaoh and said, 'My lord, when I was in prison, the chief baker and I both had strange dreams. A young Hebrew, named Joseph, who was in prison at the same time, told us what our dreams meant – and he was right.'

'Send for Joseph,' commanded Pharaoh.

So Joseph was quickly shaved and dressed in fine linen, as was the custom for those who had to appear before the great Pharaoh. He wondered what was going to happen to him.

Pharaoh said, 'I had two dreams last night and no one can tell me what they mean. But I hear that you can do so.'

Joseph said, 'I can't do it myself. I can only say what God tells me to say.'

So Pharaoh related his dreams. 'I was standing on the banks of the River Nile,' he said, 'when seven fat, healthy-looking cattle came out of the river and began to feed along the bank. Then seven more cows came up from the river, but these were skinny, hungry-looking animals. These skinny ones ate up the fat ones, but when they had eaten them, they were still as thin as before. Then I woke up. When I went to

sleep again, I had another dream. This time I saw seven full ears of corn growing on one stalk. Then seven thin, withered ears, blown by the east wind, sprouted up and seemed to swallow up the fat ones. I have told my magicians these dreams, but they can't explain what they mean.'

Then Joseph said, 'Both dreams mean the same thing. In them God is telling you what will happen to the land. There will be seven years of good harvest and plenty of food, followed by seven years of dreadful famine, so bad that the years of plenty will all be forgotten. The double dream means that this is going to happen very soon.

'I suggest you find the wisest man in all Egypt and put him in charge of the land. He should have other men under him to collect all the spare food during the seven good years and store it up for the seven bad years.'

This seemed very wise advice to Pharaoh, but where in Egypt could he find a man wise and able enough to take charge of such a big plan? Suddenly he realized that the very man for the job was Joseph himself. Pharaoh turned to him and said, 'Since God has shown you the meaning of the dreams, you are the wisest man in the country. I shall put you in charge of the palace, and everyone will do just as you say.'

Pharaoh took the ring from his finger and put it on Joseph's hand. Then he gave him some fine clothes and a gold chain to put round his neck, and his second best chariot to ride in.

Joseph set to work straight away. During the seven good years he stored up food in every city from the fields around. Then came the seven bad years when nothing seemed to grow in Egypt or in any of the lands around. Joseph's interpretation of the dreams came true, and in Egypt itself there was enough food for everyone because of the grain that Joseph had ordered to be saved.

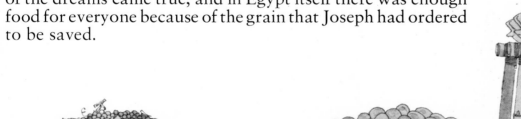

Corn in Egypt

JOSEPH'S brothers came to Egypt to buy corn during the famine. They did not know Joseph was in charge of selling the corn and did not recognize him in his fine clothes. He spoke roughly to them, through an interpreter because he did not wish them to know that he could speak their language.

'Where do you come from?' he asked.

'From the land of Canaan, to buy food,' said the brothers.

'You're spies, who have come to find out about my country,' said Joseph harshly.

'No, no, my lord!' protested the brothers. 'We've come to buy food. We are all brothers, sons of one man. Benjamin, the youngest, stayed at home with our father, and one brother is dead.'

'I want to see this youngest brother you speak of to know whether you are telling the truth,' Joseph said. 'One of you must go for him while the rest of you remain here in prison.' He put the brothers in prison for three days while they discussed what to do.

On the third day, Joseph thought of his father and all the other members of the family at home, so he sent for the brothers.

'I am a man who loves God,' he said. 'If you are honest men, let one of you stay here, while the rest go and take corn back to your families. Then you must return here with Benjamin.'

'All this trouble serves us right for what we did to Joseph,' the brothers said to each other. They did not know that Joseph could understand what they were saying, and Joseph

had to turn away from them to hide his tears. Joseph then went to his servants and said, 'Fill their sacks with corn and, without them knowing it, put back into the sacks the money which they have brought to buy corn. Give them some food for the journey too.'

One brother was kept prisoner while the rest set off back to Canaan. Long before they reached home, one of them opened his sack to feed the donkeys, and there on the top he saw his money!

'What's this?' he said, and they were all frightened and wondered what the great lord in Egypt would do if the corn was not paid for.

When they reached home, they told Jacob all that had happened to them. Then they opened all their sacks and found that every man's money was in his sack! They did not know what to do.

Jacob did not want to risk any harm coming to Benjamin and refused to let him go to Egypt.

The famine grew worse, however, and soon they had used all the corn they had bought. Jacob had to give in and Benjamin prepared to set off with his brothers.

'Take double money this time,' Jacob advised them, 'in case there was a mistake last time.'

The Silver Cup

JOSEPH'S brothers brought Benjamin, the youngest, with them when they came to Egypt for the second time. They still did not recognize Joseph who was in charge of selling the corn.

Joseph gave them a great welcome and ordered a special meal to be prepared. After the meal Joseph summoned his steward.

'Fill the men's sacks with corn,' he commanded. 'Put each man's money back in his sack with the corn and when you get to the youngest's, put my own special silver cup in as well.'

The next morning, as soon as the brothers had set off, Joseph sent for his steward again.

'Go and catch up with those men,' he said, 'and ask them why they have stolen my silver cup.'

The brothers were astonished when the steward caught up with them and accused them of stealing. They watched as he searched each sack in turn, starting with the eldest's. When the cup was discovered in Benjamin's sack they were so horrified they all agreed to go back with Benjamin and the steward to Joseph's house.

There Joseph told them that he was going to keep Benjamin as his slave but the rest of the brothers could return to their father. The brothers did not know what to do. Their father had been so reluctant to let Benjamin go to Egypt in the first place that they knew it would break his heart if Benjamin had

to remain there. So one of the brothers stepped forward and explained this to Joseph.

'Our father has already lost one son,' he ended, 'and if he loses Benjamin too he will die of grief. Let me stay as your slave instead so that Benjamin can go back home with the others.'

Joseph was so moved by this he felt he could no longer keep secret that he was the lost brother whom they had talked about. He sent everyone out of the room except his brothers and then exclaimed,

'I am Joseph! Although you sold me to Egypt you needn't be upset, for God has been able to save many people from starvation through me. Now hurry home and fetch our father and your families and animals too. You can all live here in Egypt as there are still five more years of famine to come.'

Then Joseph hugged them all and they talked together for a long time about all that had happened since Joseph had been sold to the traders.

Pharaoh was delighted with the news. 'They will be given the best land in Egypt,' he said, 'and they will have everything they need.' So Joseph and his father were happily reunited and all their relations came to live in Egypt.

Moses in the Bulrushes

THE Israelites had been living in Egypt for many years and they had become a strong and powerful race of people. The new Pharaoh was alarmed.

'These Israelites are becoming mightier than we are,' he said. 'We must deal with them before they grow dangerous.'

So Pharaoh and the Egyptians made the Israelites into slaves. They put strict taskmasters over them and forced them to make bricks to build new cities. The Israelites had to toil long and hard, carrying heavy loads. But the more they were ill-treated, the more their numbers seemed to grow.

This made Pharaoh angry and he thought up a wicked plan. He ordered the nurses to kill all the baby boys who were born to the Israelites, but the nurses refused to carry out such a cruel order.

Then Pharaoh himself spoke to the Israelites. 'Every son that is born to you,' he said, 'must be cast into the River Nile, but you may let every daughter live.'

Now there was one Israelite and his wife who already had a daughter called Miriam and who now had a new baby son. They could not bear to let him be drowned in the Nile, and they managed to keep him hidden for three months. The time came when they could hide him no longer and they had to think of a new plan.

His mother made a little basket of bulrushes (the reeds which grew along the river bank). She wove the stalks together and covered the outside with a tarry mixture to make it waterproof.

Then she put the baby into the basket, carried it down to the river and hid it among the reeds. The baby's sister, Miriam, stood a little way away to see what would happen.

Presently the princess, the daughter of Pharaoh, came down to the river with her maids to bathe. Suddenly she saw the little basket and sent one of her maids to get it. When she opened it, she saw the baby. He was crying and Pharaoh's daughter felt sorry for him even though she realized he was one of the Hebrew children.

Then Miriam came out from her hiding-place and went up to the princess and said, 'Shall I go and find a nurse from among the Hebrew women to look after the baby for you?'

The princess agreed, and clever Miriam ran off and brought back her own mother! How delighted the mother was to see her baby again!

Pharaoh's daughter said to her, 'Take the child away and look after him for me, and I will pay you your wages.'

Happily the mother took her little son and nursed him. He grew into a fine boy and, when he was big enough, she took him to Pharaoh's daughter. This was a sad moment for the mother for she knew that from now on he would live at the palace and the princess would look upon him as her own son.

'I will call him Moses,' said the princess.

Moses and the Burning Bush

ONE day Moses was out looking after his father-in-law's sheep. He was on a mountainside when suddenly a bush burst into flames.

'That's very strange,' Moses said to himself, 'the bush is alight, but it's not burning.'

As he got nearer, a voice spoke to him from the bush. It was the voice of God. He said, 'Moses! Moses! Don't come any nearer and take off your shoes, for you are standing on holy ground. I am the God of Abraham, of Isaac and of Jacob.'

Moses hid his face, for he was afraid.

Then God told him that he had seen how the Hebrews were suffering in Egypt under the new Pharaoh. 'You must be their leader and rescue them,' God said.

'Me!' said Moses. 'I can't go to Pharaoh and bring the people out of Egypt.'

To which God said, 'I will be with you. You are to tell the people God has sent you.'

'They wouldn't believe me,' said Moses.

'Throw that rod in your hand on to the ground,' said God.

Moses did so, and the rod immediately became a serpent.

'Now pick it up by the tail,' said God, which Moses did, and it became a rod again.

This was a sign to Moses that God can do wonderful things and that he must trust God.

The Plagues of Egypt

MOSES returned to Egypt with his rod in his hand, to rescue the Israelites.

His brother Aaron met him on the way, and together they went to see the new Pharaoh. They said to him, 'The Lord God of Israel says, "Let my people go."'

Pharaoh was scornful. 'Why should I listen to *him*?' he scoffed, and he ordered the taskmasters to make the Israelite slaves work even harder at building his new cities.

'Don't give them any straw to make bricks,' he said. 'Make them go and gather it themselves, and see to it that they make the same number of bricks as before.'

When Moses heard this he said to God, 'Why did you send me here? Look what's happened! The Israelites are worse off now than before.'

God told him that all would be well and that he would save his people. Moses knew he must go on trusting God, however hard it seemed but the Israelites did not find it easy to believe that God would save them.

One day God said to Moses, 'Go and wait for Pharaoh by the river and take your rod in your hand. When Pharaoh comes tell him that if he still refuses to let the Israelites go, you will strike the water with your rod, and it will become blood. The same will happen to all the rivers, canals and ponds in the land.'

This was exactly what happened, and the water became blood for a week. The Egyptians were horrified but still Pharaoh would not let the people of Israel go.

Then God sent Moses to Pharaoh with another warning. 'Let the Israelites go or the whole of your country will swarm with frogs.'

Pharaoh still refused, and out came thousands of frogs hopping about all over the land, until even Pharaoh could not bear it any longer.

'Ask God to take the frogs away,' he said to Moses and Aaron, 'and then I'll let the people go.'

As soon as God removed the frogs, Pharaoh changed his mind. He could not bear to lose all his valuable slaves.

Then God sent a plague of gnats and then a plague of flies, swarming all over the houses of the Egyptians. After that came plagues of animal disease and horrible boils which caused great suffering to the Egyptians. Each time the plague stopped, Pharaoh refused to let the Israelites go.

Next God sent a plague of hail and lightning. It crushed the crops in the fields and killed any people or animals who were outside. No one had ever seen a storm like it!

At last Pharaoh said to Moses, 'I've had enough! Ask God to stop the storm and I will let the people go.' So God made

the storms cease, but Pharaoh once more changed his mind.

'How long do you mean to defy the Lord God?' asked Moses and Aaron, who by now were tired of Pharaoh's stubbornness. 'If you refuse again, there will be a plague of locusts.'

Pharaoh remained obstinate, and down came clouds of locusts. They filled the palaces and houses of all the Egyptians, and the ground was black with them. They ate up everything growing, until not one green thing remained.

'I was wrong,' said Pharaoh. 'Forgive me just once more and ask your God to take away the locusts.'

Moses prayed to God, and God sent a strong wind to sweep the locusts away. As soon as they had all gone, Pharaoh once more said, 'I won't let the Israelites go!'

Then God sent a great darkness over all of Egypt except where the people of Israel lived. The Egyptians could not see each other and dared not leave their homes.

Pharaoh called for Moses and Aaron. 'You may go and worship the Lord,' he said, 'but leave all your animals here.'

Moses refused to leave the animals and God told Moses that he would send one final plague and after that the Israelites would be able to leave Egypt.

41

The First Passover

GOD spoke to Moses again. 'One final plague will come to the Egyptians, and then Pharaoh will let the Israelites go. At about midnight every first-born son in Egypt will die and the first-born of all the cattle too. But not one of the Israelites will die.'

God gave exact instructions as to what the Israelites were to do.

Each family was to kill a lamb, a special lamb, without blemish, and with its blood to make a mark on the door frame of the house, on the doorposts and above the door. This would show which were the houses where the Israelites lived. Then they were to roast the lamb and eat it with herbs and unleavened bread. (Unleavened bread is bread without yeast for there was no time to wait for it to rise.) They were to be wearing their shoes and travelling clothes – prepared for a journey.

If the household was too small for a whole lamb, then two neighbouring households were to share, for none of the meat must be left until the morning. No one was to be allowed out on this particular night.

The Israelites obeyed these instructions.

Then, during that night, at midnight, death came to the land of Egypt, and in every house where the door was not marked, from Pharaoh's palace to the smallest home in the land, the eldest son died.

This event was called 'The Lord's Passover' because God had said to Moses and Aaron, 'When I see the blood I will pass over you.'

What a terrible night it was! Pharaoh was really frightened this time, and he sent for Moses and Aaron and said,

'Get out all you Israelites! Leave my country and go and worship your God as you wish, but give me a blessing before you go.'

The Egyptian people were as anxious as Pharaoh to be rid of the Israelites as quickly as possible, before any more troubles fell upon them. They gave the Israelites gold and silver and clothing and whatever they asked for.

Off went the joyful Israelites! At last they were free! A great company of them set off on their journey out of Egypt. They had been in slavery in Egypt for 430 years, so none of them knew what it was like to be free.

43

Crossing the Sea

THE Israelites left Egypt in a great procession. In order to get from Egypt to the land God had promised them, they had to cross the desert and then get to the other side of the sea.

God was with them and he went before them in the form of a pillar of cloud during the day and a pillar of fire at night to give them light.

There was trouble in Egypt, for without the Israelites to serve them, the Egyptians had to do all their own work. They felt angry and grumbled to Pharaoh about it.

'Why did we let those Israelite slaves get away?' his officials asked him.

So Pharaoh decided to try to get the Israelites back. He gathered together an army, including six hundred of his fastest war chariots, and they all chased after the people of Israel.

When the Israelites saw this great army coming after them, they were terrified. The sea was in front of them and Pharaoh and his army were behind.

'Why didn't you leave us in Egypt? Look what you've done now!' they cried to Moses. 'It would have been better to be slaves in Egypt than to die here in the wilderness!'

'Don't be afraid,' said Moses. 'Just stay where you are and watch, and you will see the Lord rescue you in a wonderful way. He will fight for you!'

Then God said to Moses, 'Lift up your rod and stretch your hand over the sea and the water will divide into two. Then the people of Israel will be able to walk through it on dry land.'

The pillar of cloud moved until it was between the Israelites and the Egyptians, and it gave light for the Israelites, but made it dark for the Egyptians.

Moses stretched his rod over the sea, and the Lord drove back the sea with a strong wind. A path was opened through the sea and all the people of Israel marched along it.

Up galloped the Egyptians in pursuit, but their heavy chariot wheels began to get stuck in the mud.

God said to Moses, 'Stretch out your hand over the sea and the waters will be one again, and will cover the Egyptians and their chariots and their horsemen.' Moses did so, and the Egyptian army perished.

The Israelites sang a song of praise when they saw how God had saved them.

Manna and Quails

MOSES led the Israelites from the sea into the desert. Soon they began to grow hungry, for food was scarce and there was little to eat in the desert. 'At least we had food when we were in Egypt,' they grumbled, 'but now you've brought us into this wilderness, we shall all die of hunger.'

But God told Moses, 'I will send them food from heaven. Everyone can go out each day and gather as much as he needs, and on the sixth day each week they are to gather twice as much.'

So Moses and Aaron called a meeting and told the people what the Lord God had said. 'This will show you that it was the Lord who brought you out of Egypt,' they said, 'and that he is your God.'

That same evening, thousands of little brown birds called quails flew down all over the camp. They were the meat that God had provided, and the Israelites found them good to eat.

Next morning the ground all round the camp was wet with dew, and when the dew had gone, little thin flakes appeared on the ground. They looked like small white seeds.

'Manna?' said the people of Israel. (This means, 'What is it?')

'It is the food which God has sent you to eat,' said Moses. 'Everyone is to gather as much as he needs for his household.'

The Israelites found this new food tasted rather like biscuits made with honey and they called it manna. Some people gathered more and some less than they needed. Those who gathered more found they had nothing over at the end of the day, and those who gathered only a little found that they were not short. Each family had just enough for its needs.

In this way God fed the people of Israel for forty years until at last they arrived in the land of Canaan.

The Ten Commandments

THE people of Israel had been travelling for a long time. At last they reached a mountain called Mount Sinai, and God called Moses to climb up the mountain. There, God told him that if the people would keep his commandments, they would be his chosen people.

So Moses went down the mountain and called the leaders of the people together and told them what God had said.

Together the people answered, 'We will do everything that the Lord has said.'

Then God told Moses that in three days' time, he would come to meet the people, although a cloud would hide him from their sight. The people were to wash their clothes, and be ready for the occasion, but on no account were they to climb the mountain.

On the third day, the people gathered eagerly at the foot of the mountain, upon which appeared a thick cloud. Suddenly there was a terrific thunderstorm and a very loud trumpet blast was heard. All the people trembled.

Then Moses himself climbed the mountain, and was lost to sight in the cloud. There God gave him ten commandments written on two tablets of stone.

These were God's Ten Commandments:

1. *You shall not have any other gods but me.*
2. *You shall not worship carved images or statues.*
3. *Do not use my name lightly or for evil purposes.*
4. *You must keep the sabbath day holy and use it for a day of rest. I made the world in six days and rested on the seventh, and that is why I blessed it and made it a holy day.*
5. *Honour and respect your parents.*
6. *Do not kill.*
7. *Do not take away another person's husband or wife.*
8. *Do not steal.*
9. *Do not accuse anyone falsely or say anything untrue about them.*
10. *Do not yearn for things other people have – not their houses, or animals or slaves or anything that they own.*

Moses remained on the mountain so long that the people grew tired of waiting and asked Aaron if they could have a new god to lead them. When Moses did come down from the mountain, he found the people worshipping and dancing round a golden calf.

Moses was furious – so angry that he threw down the tablets with the commandments on them and they broke.

The next day Moses climbed the mountain again to ask God's forgiveness on behalf of the people and to receive the Ten Commandments again.

In the wilderness there was no temple building which the people could use for worship. So God told Moses to instruct the people to make a special tent or 'Tabernacle' which they could carry with them on their journey.

It was to be made of embroidered linen on a wooden frame, and they were to use the finest materials they could obtain. Inside it was to be divided into two parts by a beautiful curtain. The outer part was to be called The Holy Place and the inner one was to be called the Most Holy Place (or the Holy of Holies).

Inside this went the Ark, a special box of acacia wood covered with pure gold and containing the tablets of stone with the Ten Commandments carved on them. There were to be beautiful furnishings and fittings too, and everything was to be the very best that they could obtain.

The people used their skills and gave what they had to make the Tabernacle. Some of them were good at spinning or weaving or embroidery, others gave gold and silver to be beaten and precious stones to be polished and those who were craftsmen taught their skills to others.

On the day that the Tabernacle was finished, while all the people watched, a cloud covered the tent and the glory of the Lord filled the Tabernacle.

Rahab and the Spies

AFTER Moses died, God chose a new leader who was a wise and brave man called Joshua. God told Joshua that he would need to be strong and very courageous, but that he, God, would be with him, as he had been with Moses.

So Joshua gathered together his officers and told them that in three days' time they were to cross the River Jordan. Before they did so, however, Joshua thought it would be a good idea to find out what the land was like on the other side. He particularly wanted to know what the city of Jericho was like. So he sent out two spies, and when the spies reached Jericho, they found lodgings in the home of a woman whose name was Rahab. Her house was built on the city wall.

The king of Jericho heard that there were spies in his land, and he sent out his soldiers to arrest them. But Rahab hid the spies under the flax which was drying on her roof. When the soldiers came she sent them off on a false trail towards the gates of the city.

Then Rahab ran up to the spies on the roof. 'I've heard of all the wonderful things the Lord God has done for the people of Israel,' she said. 'Will you promise me, since I have been kind to you, that my family and I will be saved when the Israelites attack Jericho?'

The two spies gave her their promise and then Rahab brought a rope to lower them out of her window to the ground outside the city wall.

Before they left, the spies told her to tie a red cord to her window as a sign, and then no harm would come to her or to her relatives when the Israelites took the city.

When the two spies returned to Joshua they reported that Jericho would be easily taken.

The Fall of Jericho

JOSHUA and the Israelites moved on towards Jericho. They were led by the priests who were carrying the Ark of the Covenant – the box covered in gold in which the Ten Commandments were kept.

To reach the city they had first to cross the River Jordan. The people marched behind the priests, who stepped to the water's edge. Suddenly the river stopped flowing and the water began to pile up. Everybody was filled with wonder. It was like the crossing of the sea forty years before!

The priests bearing the Ark stood on dry ground in the middle of the river and waited until all the people had passed over to the other side. When this was safely done, Joshua ordered twelve stones from the Jordan to be erected as a monument.

'The monument will be a sign to our children,' he said. 'It will remind them that God dried up the water to enable us to cross the River Jordan.'

The city of Jericho was surrounded by high walls and the gates were kept tightly shut. The people wondered how they were going to get inside.

But God had a plan, and he said to Joshua, 'Every day for six days you and your soldiers will march around the city once. You will be led by seven priests, each carrying a trumpet, and behind them will go the Ark of the Covenant. On the seventh day you are to march round seven times, the priests blowing their trumpets. When they give one final mighty blast, all the people are to give a great shout – and the walls of the city will fall down flat.'

Joshua explained all this to his people, and he said, 'You must all march around in complete silence, except for the trumpets, until the day I tell you to shout. Then – *shout*!'

So for six days they all marched around the city once a day. On the seventh day, they all got up at dawn and began to march round the city seven times. At the seventh time the priests blew their trumpets, and Joshua cried, 'Shout! For the Lord has given us the city!'

And the walls of the city came crashing down!

In rushed the Israelites from all directions. Joshua had told them they were not to take anything, but any silver, gold, bronze or iron that they found was to be dedicated to God and put in the Lord's treasury.

Joshua became famous throughout the land as a great leader and a true servant of God.

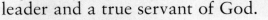

Gideon and the Midianites

THE people of Israel were afraid of the fierce Midianites who had conquered them and were to rule over them for seven years.

One day a young Israelite named Gideon was threshing some wheat in a winepress. He was working secretly so that the Midianites would not see him. Suddenly he looked up and there, sitting under an oak tree was an angel.

'The Lord is with you,' said the angel. 'He wants you to rescue Israel from the Midianites.'

'Me!' said Gideon, astounded. 'How can I? I'm nobody! I'm the least important member of a poor family.'

'The Lord will be with you,' replied the angel, 'so you'll easily be able to conquer the Midianites.'

That night Gideon had another message from God. God told him to tear down the altar to the heathen god Baal. Then Gideon was to build an altar to the Lord God in its place.

Gideon did as God asked, and soon many men flocked to join him. The day came when he and his men were ready to fight the Midianites who were camped in a valley to the north.

'You have too many soldiers,' God said to Gideon. 'They mustn't think they have conquered Midian because of their greater strength. They must understand that it is because I am with them. So give any who feel afraid the chance to return home.'

Twenty-two thousand men went back, leaving Gideon with ten thousand.

'You still have too many,' God said. 'Take them down to the water's edge to drink and I will separate them there.'

Only three hundred men scooped up the water with their hands. All the others drank with their mouths from the stream and God said they were to go home.

That night Gideon divided his three hundred men into three groups, and he gave each man a trumpet, an empty pitcher (a tall earthenware jar), and a lamp.

'When we get to the edge of the camp,' he said, 'watch me and do what I do.'

Shortly before midnight Gideon and his men reached the edge of the enemy camp. Inside their pitchers each man had hidden his lighted lamp.

Then, at a sign from Gideon, they all blew their trumpets, broke the pitchers and held up their lamps, shouting, 'The sword of the Lord and of Gideon!'

When the Midianites heard all the shouts and saw all the lights, they were terrified, and they ran away screaming, with Gideon's men chasing after them.

It was a great victory, and the Israelites were so pleased that God had helped Gideon to save them that they asked Gideon to be their ruler. Gideon answered,

'The Lord is your ruler.'

Samson

ONE of the strongest and bravest of the Israelites was a man named Samson. He was so strong that once when a lion sprang at him he killed it with his bare hands.

The Philistines had conquered the Israelites and they wanted to know the secret of Samson's great strength. Even when they tied him up with strong ropes, Samson broke out of them as easily as if they had been strands of thread.

The Philistines' chance to get the better of Samson came when he fell in love with a woman named Delilah. The Philistines bribed Delilah, saying,

'Make Samson tell you where he gets his power from and we will each give you eleven hundred pieces of silver.'

Delilah was greedy for riches and she pestered Samson with questions. At last he gave in and told her his secret. 'My hair has never been cut,' he said. 'If it were, I would lose my strength.'

Samson's mother had made a vow before he was born, that her son would be a man devoted to God's service, and that as a sign of this, he would never cut his hair.

While Samson was asleep, Delilah called for a man to come and cut off his hair and when Samson awoke he found he had lost his strength. The Philistines were now able to capture him easily and they put his eyes out. Then they chained him up and made him work in the prison.

During his time in prison, Samson's hair began to grow again.

One day the Philistines thought they would have some fun with their prisoner. They took him out of his cell and cruelly laughed at him as he wandered about blind and helpless.

'Take me to the pillars that are holding up this building,' Samson said to the boy who was leading him. Then he prayed to God, 'Lord, give me my strength once more.' He took hold of the two middle pillars, and with a hand on each of them, he pushed with all his strength and might. The building came crashing down, killing many of the Philistines who were there and killing Samson too.

Ruth

THERE was famine in the land. Elimelech and his wife Naomi, who lived in Bethlehem, decided that the only thing to do was to move to another country where they could find food for themselves and their two sons.

So they set off to walk the long journey to Moab, a foreign land where the people worshipped strange gods. When at last they arrived, they found it was a fertile and highly cultivated country. How lovely it was not to have to worry about food any more!

In time, both the sons married women of Moab, one named Ruth and the other named Orpah. This made Naomi happy, for she was very fond of her two daughters-in-law.

After about ten years, Naomi heard that the famine in her own land was over. Her husband and two sons had died and she thought it would be best if she returned home. Ruth insisted on going with her back to Bethlehem.

'Please don't say I must leave you,' she said to Naomi. 'Wherever you go, I will go; wherever you live, I will live. Your people will be my people, and your God will be my God.' So Naomi agreed to let Ruth go back with her.

When at last they reached Bethlehem, Ruth had to work in order to earn enough money to buy food for the two of them. It was harvest time and she decided to go and glean. It was the custom of the country that the reapers must leave a little of the grain round the edges of the field so that the poor might go and pick it up. This was called 'gleaning'.

Ruth gleaned in the field of a rich man named Boaz.

During the day, Boaz came to the field to see how things were getting on. He noticed Ruth. 'Who is that?' he asked one of the men.

'She's from Moab and she came back with Naomi,' replied the reaper. 'She asked if she might glean here, and she has been working hard all day.'

Boaz went over to Ruth, who was very surprised that she had been noticed, and he spoke kindly to her.

'You may always glean here,' he said. 'There is no need to go to other fields. I will see that no harm comes to you. If you are thirsty, you may drink from the water jars here.'

'But I am a foreigner,' said Ruth, bowing low. 'Why are you so kind to me?'

Boaz explained that he had heard how unselfish she had been in coming back with Naomi, and he asked her to come and have a meal with the reapers. When work started again Boaz quietly asked his men to let some extra corn fall on purpose so that there might be more for Ruth to glean.

When Ruth came home that evening with so much corn, Naomi was delighted. When she heard that Ruth had been working in a field belonging to Boaz, she was very surprised.

'But he is one of our relatives!' she exclaimed. 'Do as he says, stay with his maidens right through the harvest and I know you will be safe.'

So Ruth went on gleaning in Boaz's field all through the wheat harvest and all through the barley harvest, and she and Boaz came to know one another very well.

Naomi was delighted when Ruth told her that she and Boaz were to be married.

The Lord blessed the marriage, and one day Ruth had a son called Obed. Many years later Obed's grandson became King David.

God calls Samuel

THERE was once a good woman named Hannah. Hannah might have been very happy except for the fact that she had no children.

One day when she was in the temple, she began to cry bitterly as she prayed to God to give her a son.

'If you give me a son,' she prayed, 'I will dedicate him to you for his whole life.'

Eli, the priest of the temple was watching her as she prayed so earnestly, though he could not hear her words. Then he said to her,

'May God answer your prayers.' Hannah went home feeling much happier. Some time later, God answered her prayers and she had a baby son. She called him Samuel.

She did not forget her promise to God and, when Samuel was old enough, she took him to the temple to give him to God for his service.

She said to Eli, 'Here is the little son which God gave me in answer to my prayers. I have brought him here as I promised God, and as long as he lives, Samuel will belong to the Lord.'

Samuel stayed with Eli and learnt how to help in the temple services. When he had been at the temple some time, a strange and wonderful thing happened. One night, when the services for the day were over, Eli, who was now old and nearly blind, was sleeping in his own room, while Samuel slept in the sanctuary near the Ark of the Covenant. Apart from the lamp, which always burnt before the Ark in the temple, it was quite dark.

Suddenly Samuel heard someone call his name.

'Samuel! Samuel!' said the voice.

It must be Eli calling, thought Samuel, and he got up quickly and ran to the old priest.

'Yes! Here I am,' he said, 'what do you wish me to do?'

'But I didn't call you,' said Eli. 'Go back to bed.'

A little later, Samuel heard the voice again, so he hurried to Eli. 'You did call me,' he said, 'and I am here.'

'No I didn't,' said Eli. 'Go and lie down again.'

Puzzled, Samuel went back to bed. Then he heard the voice for the third time, and once again went to Eli.

This time Eli said, 'Go and lie down and if the voice calls again you must say, "Speak, Lord, for I am listening."'

Samuel returned to bed and the voice did call him again, and this time Samuel replied as Eli had told him.

God told him that Eli's two sons had behaved very wickedly, and were not fit to take Eli's place as priests of the temple. They would have to be punished. Next morning Samuel had the sad task of giving Eli God's message.

'He is the Lord,' said Eli. 'He will do as he knows best.'

As he grew up, Samuel received many messages from God. People listened when he spoke God's words to them, and they knew that Samuel was one of God's prophets.

David and Goliath

KING SAUL was the first king of the Israelites. He was a good king until he turned away from God and grew selfish and ill-tempered.

God asked his prophet Samuel to anoint a new king. The future king was only a boy when Samuel came to him, and his name was David. He was the youngest of eight sons and spent much of his time minding his father's sheep.

The Israelites were at war with the Philistines, and their armies were camped on opposite sides of the Valley of Elah.

Every day a huge man named Goliath came out from the Philistine camp to challenge the Israelites. The Israelites had never seen such a frightening-looking man before! He was dressed in heavy bronze armour and wore a big bronze helmet. He carried a great thick javelin and his armour-bearer walked ahead of him carrying an enormous shield.

This giant strode out and roared across the valley to the Israelites, 'What are all you men doing there? One of you must come and fight me! If he kills me, we will be your slaves, but if I win, then you will be our slaves. I dare you to send someone to fight me!'

The Israelites were terrified!

David's three eldest brothers were in Saul's army, while David stayed at home looking after the sheep. One day his father said,

'David, take this food to your brothers and find out how they are getting on, and what they are doing.'

So David went to the Israelite camp. While he was talking to his brothers, Goliath came out and shouted his usual challenge. Most of the Israelites ran away in terror, but David went to King Saul.

'Your Majesty!' he said, 'I'll go and fight this Philistine.'

'You! That's impossible,' said Saul. 'You're just a boy and he's been a mighty soldier all his life.'

'But, your Majesty,' persisted David, 'I look after my father's sheep. I've often had to kill lions and bears when they attack the sheep – and I'll do the same to this Philistine. God saved me from the lions and bears, and God will save me from Goliath!'

When King Saul saw how determined David was, he agreed to let him go. David refused to wear any armour. He took his shepherd's stick and his catapult. He chose some smooth stones from the brook, and set off to meet Goliath.

As soon as Goliath saw David, he burst into scornful laughter.

'Do you think you can beat me with a stick like a dog?' he scoffed.

David answered, 'You have come with weapons but I come to you in the name of the Lord God of Israel.'

At this Goliath rushed furiously towards David. David took out a stone from his bag, put it in his sling and hurled it straight at Goliath. It hit him on the forehead, and Goliath collapsed and crashed to the ground. He was dead. David ran forward and cut off Goliath's head with the giant's own sword.

When the Philistines saw what had happened to their champion, they turned and fled, and the Israelites chased after them, shouting about their victory.

David the Shepherd

KING DAVID ruled for forty years and was a very wise ruler. He was also a poet and a musician. One well known psalm was inspired by David's boyhood as a shepherd.

The shepherd led his sheep to green pastures and cool waters, and took care of them in rough and rocky places. At night he saw them all safely into the sheepfold. The good shepherd loved each of his sheep. God loves and takes care of each of us.

The Lord is my shepherd; I have everything I need.

He lets me rest in fields of green grass and leads me to quiet pools of fresh water.

He gives me new strength. He guides me in the right paths as he has promised.

Even if I go through the deepest darkness, I will not be afraid, Lord, for you are with me. Your shepherd's rod and staff protect me.

You prepare a banquet for me, where all my enemies can see me; you welcome me as an honoured guest and fill my cup to the brim.

I know that your goodness and love will be with me all my life; and your house will be my home as long as I live.

PSALM 23

Solomon's Wisdom

WHEN King David died, his son Solomon became King of Israel. Solomon did his best to love and obey God as his father had taught him.

One night Solomon had a dream. In it, it seemed that God was asking him what gift he would like most.

'Give me the wisdom to be a good ruler,' said Solomon, 'and to know the difference between good and evil.'

God was pleased with this request, and he said, 'Because you have asked for wisdom, instead of long life for yourself, or riches, or victory over your enemies, I will do what you ask. I will give you more wisdom and understanding than anyone has ever had before, and I will also give you the riches and honour for which you did not ask.'

Soon after that dream, two women came to Solomon for his judgement. One of the women was holding a baby in her arms and she said to him,

'Your Majesty, we both live in the same house, and we both had babies nearly the same age. One night, this woman's baby died. She took mine and said it was hers, and gave the dead baby to me.'

The other woman cried out, 'It was *her* baby who died, not mine.' They began to argue in front of the King.

'Bring me a sword,' Solomon commanded. When the sword was brought, he said, 'Divide the living child in two and give them half each.'

'No! No!' cried the real mother, who loved her baby. 'I'd rather you gave it to her than kill the child!'

'Go on!' said the second woman. 'Cut it in two.'

Then Solomon said, 'Put away the sword. Don't kill the baby. Give it to the one who spoke first. It is obvious she truly loves the child. She is its real mother.'

When the people of Israel heard about Solomon's judgement, they knew what great wisdom God had given him.

Solomon's Temple

'WE can't hear any hammering,' said some people as they watched a beautiful new temple being built in Jerusalem. What a wonderful building it was going to be!

'No, you won't hear anything,' replied another spectator, 'because all the stones are being prepared far away in the quarry, so that there will be no noise of hammers, axes or other iron tools heard in God's temple.'

In the quarry there were 80,000 men quarrying the stones, and another 70,000 men hauling the stones to Jerusalem. The building of the temple would take seven years.

One of Solomon's good friends was Hiram, King of Tyre, and Solomon asked Hiram to lend him some skilled wood-cutters.

Hiram was delighted to help and he sent his friend cedar and pine trees too.

The temple was to be three storeys high. The inside walls were covered with cedar wood and the floor with pine, and there was a coating of gold over the whole of the inside.

There was a main room, and an inner room called the Most Holy Place, where the Ark of the Covenant was kept. In the Most Holy Place there were two cherubim made of olive wood and covered with gold. They were over four metres tall, and their outstretched wings touched each other in the middle of the room and rose over the Ark.

All the walls of the main room and of the Most Holy Place were covered with carvings of cherubim, flowers and palm-trees.

At the entrance to the temple were two huge bronze columns, each eight metres tall, and decorated with a design of chains and fruit with lilies at the top. These columns were given names. The one on the south side was named Jachin, which means 'God will support', and the one on the north was named Boaz, which means 'In God is strength'.

There were lots of other furnishings in the temple – a circular bronze tank to hold water for the priests to use, ten

basins for washing the animal sacrifices, ten gold lampstands and a hundred gold bowls. Everything was perfectly made, for nothing but the best is good enough for God.

At last, after seven years' work, it was all finished. The temple stood gleaming gloriously in the sunlight. Then, with all the people gathered together, Solomon stood before the altar and praised God and asked for his blessing on the people.

Elijah and the Widow

WHEN Solomon died, his people were divided into two kingdoms – the southern kingdom of Judah and the northern kingdom of Israel.

A severe drought came to the land, and there was no rain for several years. This was the time when God sent a great and mighty prophet named Elijah to the land.

One day God said to Elijah, 'Go to the brook of Cherith, and there you will have water to drink. I have also ordered ravens to bring you food there.'

So Elijah went and camped by the brook of Cherith, and ravens brought him bread and meat to eat, and he drank from the brook.

Before long, however, even the brook dried up because there was still no rain anywhere in the land.

Then God said to Elijah, 'Go to the town of Zarephath, near Sidon, for I have asked a widow there to feed you.'

Elijah obeyed and set off. When he came near to the gate of the town, he saw a woman gathering sticks.

He called out to her, 'Please would you bring me a drink of water?' As she was going to get it, he added, 'And some bread too, please.'

Now because of the drought and famine in the land, both water and bread were very scarce.

'I'm sorry, but I have no bread,' the woman said to him. 'All I have left is a handful of flour and a little oil in a jar. I was just gathering a few sticks for a fire to cook it for myself and my son. After we have eaten it, we are sure to starve.'

'Don't worry,' said Elijah. 'Go and do as you have said. But first bake a small loaf from what you have and bring it to me, and then bake for yourself and your son. God has promised that you will have plenty of flour and oil until the day he sends rain.'

The widow had faith and trusted God's word, and so she baked the bread and used the oil. Afterwards each time she went back to her containers, she found flour and oil in them. They always had enough to eat, no matter how much they used.

One day, the widow's son became very ill, and though his mother did all she could, the boy got worse and died. In great distress she cried to Elijah,

'Have you come here to punish my sins by killing my son?'

She was so upset that she hardly knew what she was saying.

'Give the boy to me,' Elijah replied, and he took the boy from her and carried him upstairs and laid him on the bed. Then he prayed and asked God for his help.

He stretched himself over the boy three times and prayed, 'O Lord my God, let this child's spirit come back to him!'

God heard Elijah's prayer, and the boy revived and sat up. He was quite well again! Elijah took him downstairs to his mother.

'See! Your son is alive!' he said joyfully.

The widow was full of happiness. She looked at Elijah and said, 'Now I know for sure that you are God's prophet, and that the Lord really speaks through you.'

Elijah on Mount Carmel

FOR a long time there had been no rain in the land. The crops would not grow and there was hardly any grass for the cattle to eat.

One day, God said to Elijah, 'Go to Ahab the king, and I will send rain on the earth.'

So Elijah set off and when Ahab saw him he said,

'So you are the man who has brought all this trouble on the land.'

Elijah said firmly, 'No, it is your fault for disobeying God's laws and worshipping Baal, the heathen god. Order the people of Israel to meet me on Mount Carmel, and bring all the prophets of your god Baal, and I will show you which is the true God.'

The king did as Elijah had said, and crowds of people, together with all the prophets of Baal, came to Mount Carmel to see what would happen.

Elijah glared round at them all and said, 'How long will it be before you decide which is the true God? If the Lord is God, then follow him, but if Baal is your god, then follow Baal.'

No one answered him so he went on,

'I am the only prophet of the Lord now, but there are four hundred and fifty prophets of Baal. Fetch two bulls. The prophets of Baal shall choose one and lay it on the wood for a sacrifice, without lighting a fire under the wood. I will do the same with the other. Then we will each call upon our god to send down fire, and the god who answers by sending fire is the true god.'

'Well said!' shouted the people.

Elijah turned to the prophets of Baal. 'You first,' he said, 'for there are many of you.'

The prophets of Baal arranged the wood and prepared the bull for burning. Then they began calling upon their god. 'Baal! Baal! Answer us!'

All morning they continued shouting, but nothing happened. Then they leapt and danced round the altar, but still there was no sign from Baal.

About midday, Elijah made fun of them. 'Shout louder,' he said. 'Perhaps your god is sleeping or has gone away!'

So they cried all the louder, and even cut themselves with their knives in their frenzy, but still there was not a spark of fire to be seen.

The prophets of Baal went on shouting and raving all afternoon until at last they grew too tired to shout any more.

Then Elijah called all the people to him and they watched him build up the altar with stones and dig a wide trench round it. Then he piled up the wood and put the bull on top.

'Now fill four jars of water and pour them over the sacrifice and the wood,' he said.

Elijah ordered this to be done three times until the water ran all over the altar and filled the trench.

Then Elijah walked to the altar and prayed, 'O Lord God, show these people that you are the God of Israel and that I am your servant, and that I have done all these things at your command.'

Suddenly, there came a flash of fire. In spite of all the water, the flames took hold and burnt up the wood and the bull. All the water in the trench was dried up.

When the people saw this, they fell down on their faces and cried, 'The Lord, he is God!'

After this Elijah took his servant and climbed to the top of Mount Carmel, where he knelt and prayed.

Then he said to his servant, 'Go and look out to sea for signs of rain.' When the servant returned he said he had not seen any clouds.

Elijah ordered him to go again and again and when he came back the seventh time, he said, 'I saw a little cloud no bigger than a man's hand.'

In a little while, the sky grew black, the wind blew, and great splashes of rain began to fall! How thankful the people were! The drought was now over!

Naboth's Vineyard

NEAR to King Ahab's palace was a beautiful vineyard owned by a man called Naboth. Ahab wanted Naboth's vineyard for himself, so he said to Naboth,

'Either sell me your vineyard or let me exchange it for a better one.'

'No,' said Naboth. 'That land has been in my family for many years. I cannot let it go.'

This made Ahab very angry. He stormed back to the palace and sulked. Then he went to bed and refused to eat.

Jezebel, his wicked wife, came to see what was wrong. When Ahab explained she said,

'Are you the King of Israel or are you not? Don't be silly! Get up and have some food, and I will see that you get Naboth's vineyard.'

She went away and wrote letters in Ahab's name to the city leaders of Jezreel where Naboth lived. The letters said, 'Call all the people together and find two dishonest men to say in public that Naboth has cursed God and the King. Then you must have him stoned to death.'

The city leaders were afraid to disobey, and they carried out the instructions. Soon the Queen received a message that Naboth was dead.

Jezebel went to her husband. 'You can have Naboth's vineyard now,' she said. 'He is dead.'

So Ahab went to claim the vineyard.

God spoke to the prophet Elijah and told him to meet Ahab in the vineyard.

When Ahab saw Elijah, he said, 'Have you found me out?'

'I have,' said Elijah sternly. 'Because you have done wrong in God's sight, evil will come to you. All your possessions will be taken from you, and your wife Jezebel will die, because she ordered Naboth's death.'

When Ahab heard this, he was sorry for what he had done.

Then God spoke again to Elijah. 'Because Ahab is sorry for what he has done, I will forgive him.'

The Chariot of Fire

ELIJAH'S work as God's prophet was coming to an end, and someone else had to be found to take his place.

One day old Elijah was walking through the fields when he found the young man who was to be his successor. His name was Elisha, and he was busy ploughing a field with a team of oxen.

Elijah went up to him and put his own cloak round Elisha's shoulders. Elisha knew that this was a sign to him that he must carry on Elijah's work of telling the people to serve and worship God.

Elisha loved his own family dearly so he said to Elijah,

'Let me go back and say good-bye to my father and mother, and then I will come with you.'

Elijah agreed and, after his farewells, Elisha left his home to follow Elijah.

One day Elijah said to Elisha,

'You stay here, for God has ordered me to go to Bethel.'

Elisha refused to leave him, and when Elijah was sent by God to Jericho and then to Jordan, Elisha insisted on going with him.

When they reached the River Jordan, a group of about fifty prophets who had followed them from Bethel stood a short distance away, waiting to see what would happen. In some way, they knew that Elijah was to be taken away from them.

Elijah asked Elisha, 'What would you like me to do for you before I am taken away from you?'

Elisha answered, 'Let me have a double share of your spirit.'

'That's a hard thing to ask,' said Elijah, 'but you will have it if you see me as I am being taken away from you.'

They continued to walk along together and suddenly a chariot of fire drawn by horses came between them, and it took Elijah up to heaven in a great whirlwind.

Elisha saw it and gave a great shout. Then he picked up Elijah's cloak and struck the river with it, as he had seen his master do when they first arrived at the Jordan. The water parted and he walked over on dry land to the other side.

The fifty prophets saw this wonderful thing happen and they said, 'The power of Elijah is now on Elisha!' And they bowed before him.

Elisha carried on the work of God's prophet for more than fifty years, preaching the word of God to all the people.

Naaman the Leper

THE countries of Israel and Syria were often at war with one another, and each side took prisoners from the other.

Naaman was the commander-in-chief of the Syrian army. He was a very great leader, and he had led his troops to many victories. The King of Syria thought very highly of him.

One day, in one of the border raids into Israel, the Syrians captured a young slave girl. She was taken as a maid to Naaman's wife. The little captured slave girl noticed that despite his success, Naaman was not a happy man. She soon discovered the reason. Naaman was suffering from a dreaded skin disease known as leprosy for which there was hardly any hope of a cure.

One day the girl said to her mistress, 'How I wish my master would go and see the prophet Elisha who is in Samaria! I know he could cure him.'

Naaman was eager to go for he could not let any hope of a cure pass.

The King agreed, so Naaman set out, taking with him gifts of silver, gold and fine clothing, and a letter from the King of Syria to the King of Israel.

The letter read, 'The man bringing this letter is my servant Naaman, and I want you to have him cured of his leprosy.'

When the King of Israel read it, he was furious.

'Who does the King of Syria think I am?' he shouted. 'Am I God that I decide who should live and who should die? This is just an excuse to start a quarrel with me so that he can invade our land again.'

Elisha heard about the King's anger, and he sent a message to him saying, 'Let this man Naaman come to me, and I will show him that there is a prophet in Israel!'

So Naaman set off with his chariot and horses and stopped at the door of Elisha's house. He quite expected that Elisha

would come out and greet him. But all that happened was that Elisha's servant came out with a message saying, 'My master says you are to go and wash in the River Jordan seven times and you will be cured.'

This made Naaman very angry. 'At least I thought the prophet would have come out to see me,' he fumed. 'I expected him to call upon his God, and lay his hand on my sores! Why should I wash in the Jordan? Aren't our rivers in Damascus better than any river here?'

He stalked away crossly. But his servants tried to make him see sense.

'If the prophet had asked you to do something hard, sir,' they said, 'wouldn't you have done it? So why not obey when he asks you to do something as simple as this?'

Naaman saw that this was reasonable. He went to the River Jordan and washed himself in it seven times. And his flesh became as healthy as a child's and he was completely cured!

He went straight back to Elisha to thank him.

'Now I know that there is no god in all the world but the God of Israel,' he said to Elisha. 'Please accept a gift from me.' Elisha refused the gift, for he knew it was not his own power but God's which had cured Naaman.

Naaman then asked for two mule-loads of earth to take back with him. In those days people thought that each country had its own god who could only be worshipped on that country's soil.

'I will build an altar in Syria on this soil from Israel,' he said, 'so I can worship the God of Israel all my days.'

The Fiery Furnace

THE Babylonians had fought against Judea and carried off many Jews into captivity in Babylon. The King of Babylon was Nebuchadnezzar, and he felt so important and proud of himself that he thought everyone should worship him instead of the true God.

He had an enormous golden statue made, 27 metres high and nearly 3 metres wide, and he decided to have a grand ceremony to dedicate it. He called together all the important people in the land and they all stood round the great statue.

A herald stepped forward and announced in a loud voice, 'People of all nations, when you hear the sound of the musical instruments, you are commanded to fall down and worship the golden statue that the king has set up. Anyone who does not will immediately be thrown into a burning fiery furnace.'

As soon as the people heard the music, they fell to the ground and worshipped the golden statue – all except three young Jews. Their names were Shadrach, Meshach and Abednego.

Immediately some Babylonians went and reported to the king that these three had disobeyed his orders.

The king flew into a furious rage.

'Bring them to me!' he thundered. When they stood before him he told them that if they refused to worship the statue they would immediately be cast into a burning fiery furnace.

'Your Majesty,' replied the three young Jews, 'our God whom we serve is able to save us from the fire, but even if he does not, we shall still refuse to worship your god and we shall not bow down to the golden statue.'

'Make the furnace seven times hotter than usual!' the king commanded. 'Bind these three men up and throw them in.'

So Shadrach, Meshach and Abednego were tied up and thrown, fully clothed, into the roaring flames. The fire was so fierce that the flames leapt out and burnt the soldiers who were throwing the prisoners into it.

Nebuchadnezzar, standing well back, looked into the fire and was astonished to see four men walking about in the fire. The fourth one looked like a god.

Then Nebuchadnezzar went as close as he could and called out, 'Shadrach, Meshach and Abednego! You who serve the Most High God! Come out of the fire!'

The three friends walked out, unharmed. The flames had not touched them. Their hair was not singed, their clothes were not scorched. There was not even a smell of burning.

King Nebuchadnezzar said, 'Praise to the God of Shadrach, Meshach and Abednego, who sent his angel to save his servants who trusted in him. Now I make a new decree. Anyone who speaks against the God of Shadrach, Meshach and Abednego, will be utterly destroyed, for there is no god more powerful than theirs.'

Daniel in the Lions' Den

THE Persians overthrew the great Babylonian Empire and the new king was Darius the Mede. King Darius liked Daniel who was one of the captured Jews and put him in charge of the governors. The governors were jealous of him and wanted him to lose his good job. They did their best to find fault with him, but they could not, for Daniel did nothing wrong or dishonest. So they hatched a plot.

'As we can't find anything wrong with his work,' they said to each other, 'let us see if we can get him into trouble about the God he worships. He doesn't worship our gods!'

So they plotted secretly and then they went to King Darius.

'Your Majesty,' they said, 'we have come to ask you to make a new law. For the next thirty days, anyone who asks anything of any god or any man except you, shall be thrown into a den of lions.'

The king was flattered and he signed the new law.

Daniel knew about the new law, but he also knew that it would be wrong not to continue to pray to the true God as he had always done each day. So he went as usual to his room, with its windows open towards Jerusalem. He knelt down three times a day, asking for God's help and thanking him for all he did.

Daniel's enemies were spying on him, and when they saw him at prayer, they ran off with great glee to tell the king.

'Daniel does not respect your law,' they said, 'for we have seen him praying to his God three times a day, just as he has always done.'

Now the king was upset when he heard this, and began to wonder how he could possibly save Daniel from the lions. He thought about it all day, but he could not think of any way to rescue Daniel.

In the evening, he had to give the order for the arrest, or he would have been disobeying his own new law. As Daniel was being thrown into the den of lions, the King said to him,

'May your God, whom you worship so faithfully, save you!'

A big stone was put over the mouth of the pit, and the king sealed it with his royal seal so that no one could break in and rescue Daniel.

Then King Darius went back to his palace with a sad heart. He could not eat and he spent a sleepless night worrying about what was happening to Daniel.

At dawn next morning, he got up and hurried over to the den.

'Daniel! Daniel!' he called out in a trembling voice. 'Was your God able to save you from the lions?'

To the king's great relief, the voice of Daniel said,

'Long live Your Majesty! God sent an angel to shut the lions' mouths so they did not hurt me.'

The king was delighted. He ordered his men to pull Daniel out of the pit at once. Everyone saw that he had not been harmed because he trusted in God.

Then the king made another law which said. 'In every part of my kingdom, everyone will worship Daniel's God. Daniel's God is the living God, whose power shall never come to an end. He performs great miracles and it is he who saved Daniel from the lions!'

Jonah runs away

ONE day God sent a message to a man called Jonah, asking him to go to the city of Nineveh and to warn the people there that God would punish them for their wrong-doings. Jonah did not want to go. 'I am afraid to go to that dreadful place,' he thought.

He went down to the seaport of Joppa. When he saw a ship was about to sail for Tarshish – in the opposite direction from Nineveh – he paid his fare and boarded the boat.

He climbed down into the dark hold, thinking he was hiding away from God, and before long he went to sleep.

Soon a terrific storm blew up and it looked as though everyone on board would be drowned. The wind lashed the waves and the ship tossed to and fro. The storm was so fierce that the sailors thought the vessel would be dashed to pieces. They threw the cargo overboard in order to lighten the ship, and they began to pray to their own gods.

Jonah was still down in the hold, fast asleep, and the captain hurried to awaken him.

'What are you doing down here?' he cried. 'Get up and pray to your god like everyone else is doing, and if he wills it, perhaps he can save us.'

The sailors felt that the storm must be someone's fault, so they decided to draw lots to see who was to blame. They did so, and Jonah's name was drawn.

'Who are you?' they demanded. 'Where do you come from? What have you done to bring this storm upon us?'

'I am a Hebrew,' said Jonah, 'and I worship God who made the sea and the dry land, but now I am running away from him because I am scared.'

The sailors were frightened – and the storm was getting worse.

'What an awful thing to do! How can we stop the storm?' they asked.

'Take me and throw me overboard,' said Jonah miserably. 'Then the seas will calm down again. I know this is all my fault.'

At first the sailors would not agree, and they rowed harder than ever to reach the shore but at last they had to give in.

They prayed to God and asked him not to punish them for Jonah's death, and then they took Jonah to the side of the boat and pushed him into the sea.

The storm stopped! This frightened the sailors so much that they offered sacrifices and made vows to serve Jonah's God.

They sailed peacefully on to Tarshish, while Jonah was left floundering in the sea. The water nearly choked him and the seaweed wrapped itself round his head. He wondered how long it would be before he drowned. Suddenly a great fish swam up to him and swallowed him whole in one huge gulp!

Jonah was inside the fish for three days and three nights, and he had plenty of time to think how wrong he had been to disobey God. He prayed to God and said how sorry he was and he vowed that if his life was spared he would never try to run away from God again.

All this time the fish was swimming nearer and nearer to the shore, and when it reached the land, it coughed Jonah up on to the beach.

Jonah's Second Chance

BEFORE long, Jonah knew that God was giving him another chance. God was again telling him to go to Nineveh.

'Go to Nineveh, that great city,' said God, 'and warn them as I told you before.'

Jonah had learnt his lesson so this time he did not disobey. Nineveh was such a big city that it took three days to walk through it. When Jonah had been walking for one day, he cried, 'In forty days Nineveh will be destroyed!'

The people believed that Jonah had brought the message from God, and they were very sorry for the wicked things they had been doing. The king ordered that everyone should show signs of their mourning and sorrow. They had to dress in sackcloth and even he took off his royal robes, and put on sackcloth and sat in ashes. No one was allowed to eat or drink.

The king said, 'Everyone must pray earnestly to God and must give up his wicked ways. Then perhaps God will see that we are really sorry and he will not destroy us.'

And God saw that they were truly sorry for the evil they had done, and he forgave them and their city was not destroyed.

Jonah should have been pleased that the people had repented and were saved, but instead he was angry. He felt that he had been made to look silly because God had not destroyed the city after all.

He complained to God and said, 'I thought this would happen when you first told me to come here. That's why I tried to run away to Tarshish. I knew you were a loving and merciful God, full of kindness. I knew you would decide not to punish these people. You can take my life away, Lord, for I would be better off dead.'

'What right have you to be angry like this?' asked God.

Jonah went outside the city and sulked. He made himself a little shelter from the hot sun and sat watching to see what would happen to Nineveh.

God made a plant to grow up over Jonah to give him more shade, and Jonah was very grateful. But next morning a worm ate through the stem of the plant so that it withered and died.

When the sun came up it beat down upon Jonah again and a scorching east wind blew, so that Jonah once more began to wish he were dead.

Then God said, 'Do you think it right for you to be angry about the plant?'

Jonah thought he had every right to be angry.

God said, 'Is it right to be angry about a plant which grew up and withered in one night when you did nothing to help it grow? I should be much more sorry for Nineveh where there are one hundred and twenty thousand of my people as well as animals!'

Then Jonah understood that God was right to show love and mercy to the people whom he had made.

The New Testament

The Birth of John the Baptist

THE old priest Zechariah was alone burning incense in the temple. Suddenly he saw an angel standing by the side of the altar, and he felt very frightened.

'Don't be afraid,' said the angel. 'God has heard your prayers, and your wife Elisabeth is to have a son, and you are to name him John. He will be filled with God's Holy Spirit and will go as God's messenger, preparing the way for the Lord.'

Zechariah couldn't believe it. 'How shall I know if this is so?' he asked. 'My wife and I are both old.'

So the angel answered, 'I am Gabriel. It was God who sent me to tell you this good news. Until the promise comes true, you will be silent and not able to speak.'

The weeks went by. At last Elisabeth's baby was born. It was a boy, just as the angel had promised Zechariah.

Everyone thought the baby would be called Zechariah, after his father. But to their surprise Elisabeth said, 'No! His name will be John.'

'John?' asked their friends. 'But why? You haven't any relatives with that name.'

Then they made signs to the baby's father, who still could not speak, asking him what name he wanted for the baby.

Zechariah made a sign to ask them to bring him a writing tablet and he wrote, 'His name is John'.

As soon as Zechariah had written the baby's name, he found that he could speak again.

The first thing he did was to give praise to God.

The First Christmas

IN the little village of Nazareth in Galilee there lived a gentle young woman whose name was Mary. She was humble and always did her best to obey God's laws. She was engaged to a good kind man named Joseph. Joseph was a carpenter, and his family were descended from King David.

One day the Angel Gabriel appeared to Mary.

'You are greatly favoured,' he said. 'The Lord is with you. You are blessed among women.' Puzzled and rather frightened, Mary wondered what this could mean.

'Don't be afraid, Mary,' continued the angel, 'for God has blessed you in a very special way. You are going to have a baby boy and you are to call him Jesus. He will be great and his kingdom will never end.'

'How can this happen?' asked Mary. 'I have no husband.'

'God's Holy Spirit will come to you,' replied Gabriel, 'and your baby will be the son of God.'

Mary bowed her head humbly and said, 'I am God's servant, and I am willing to do whatever he wants.'

An angel also appeared to Joseph and told him about the holy child who was to be born to Mary.

'His name is to be Jesus and he will be the saviour, for he will save people from their sins,' said the angel.

At that time the country formed part of the Roman Empire, and the emperor ordered everyone to go to the place where he had been born. There he was to have his name registered so that he could be taxed. People who had left their home town must return to it, and for Joseph this meant a journey of several days back to Bethlehem.

Joseph and Mary set off on their long and tiring journey. When they reached Bethlehem, they found the place was crowded with people who had come to have their names registered. All the inns were full, and they could not find a spare room anywhere.

One innkeeper, however, felt very sorry when he saw how tired Mary looked, and he said kindly,

'I'm afraid I have no room in my inn, but you can take shelter in the stable if you wish.'

They accepted thankfully, and Mary and Joseph settled for the night among the animals and the hay.

During the night, the wonderful event happened. Mary's son was born. She lovingly wrapped him in swaddling clothes as was the custom in those days with new-born babies. There was no proper cradle for him, so she laid him gently in the manger where they kept the hay for the animals' food.

The Shepherds

IN the fields outside Bethlehem a group of shepherds were guarding their sheep one night. It was a dark night but the stars were shining brightly. The shepherds were alert listening for any wild animals which might be prowling round ready to attack the sheep.

Suddenly, the sky became full of a brilliant light making the hills and fields gloriously bright. In the midst of the light they saw an angel standing.

The shepherds were so terrified that they fell to the ground covering their faces.

'Don't be frightened,' said the angel, 'for I have come to bring you joyful news for everyone in the world. Tonight in Bethlehem, the Messiah, the Saviour of the world, has been born. You will recognize him, for you will find a baby, wrapped in swaddling clothes, lying in a manger.'

Then the angel was joined by hosts of other angels, all praising God and singing,

'Glory to God in the highest, and on earth peace among men with whom he is pleased.'

Then the bright light began to fade and the angels disappeared. The only lights left were the stars.

The shepherds looked at one another in wonder. Could this really be true? The Messiah – in Bethlehem?

'Come on,' they said to one another. 'Let's go to Bethlehem and see this wonderful thing which has happened, which the Lord has told us about.'

They ran off hastily towards the town. They knew what they were looking for – not a king in a palace, not a child in a house, but a baby in a manger.

When they got to Bethlehem, it did not take them long to find Mary and Joseph in the stable at the inn, with the wonderful new baby lying on the hay in the manger.

The shepherds were so excited that they could not keep the news to themselves. They told everyone they met afterwards how they had found the baby, and how the angel had told them that he was the Messiah they had been awaiting. The people who listened to them were amazed. They could not understand such a story. It did not seem possible that the Messiah could be born in a stable.

The shepherds had no doubts about what they had heard and seen. They went back to their flocks praising God for all that had happened.

The Wise Men

SOON after the birth of Jesus, far away in the east some wise men had been studying the stars. They were excited by a new bright star which had appeared in the sky. According to their understanding, this meant that a new king of the Jews had been born in a country thousands of miles away.

The Jews had long been expecting a new leader – a Messiah – and the wise men believed that this new king had been sent by God.

'We must go and find him and worship him,' they said.

So they prepared themselves and their camels for a very long journey, and they collected gifts fit for a king.

After many months of travelling, guided by the star, they arrived in Jerusalem where Herod was reigning as King of Judea.

'Where is the baby who is born to be King of the Jews?' asked the wise men.

When it came to Herod's ears that they were asking about a new king, he was very upset. A new king? He could not allow that so Herod sent for the wise men and said,

'Go and search carefully for the child. When you have found him, come back and tell me so that I may go and worship him too.'

Now Herod had no intention of going to worship a rival king. All he wanted was to find out as much as he could and then, if necessary, destroy the baby.

The wise men were guided by the star to Bethlehem. Then the star stopped over the house where the new king was.

The wise men were overjoyed when they at last found the young Jesus, and Mary his mother. They knelt down and worshipped him. Then they gave him their presents. One had brought gold, a rich gift suitable for a king. Another brought frankincense, a sweet-scented gum which was used to make fragrant smoke while people worshipped. The third had brought myrrh, which was a costly perfume used in medicine.

God warned the wise men in a dream not to return to Herod, but to take another route back to their own country. When Herod realized that he had been tricked, he was furious. He was determined to get rid of the new king, so he made a wicked and cruel order that all baby boys, of two years old and under, were to be killed. That way, he thought, he would surely kill the new king.

Joseph had a dream in which an angel came to him and told him to take Mary and Jesus and to go and hide in Egypt. They went to Egypt and were safe there until King Herod's death. Then the angel came again to Joseph and told him when they could return home. Instead of going back to Judea, they settled in their home town of Nazareth.

Jesus as a Boy

FORTY days after Jesus' birth, Mary and Joseph took him to Jerusalem. The law said that the first-born son of any Jewish family had to be presented to the Lord and that a sacrifice of a pair of doves or two young pigeons should also be offered.

There lived at Jerusalem an old man named Simeon. God had told Simeon he would not die until he had seen the Messiah. He was in the temple on the day when Mary and Joseph came with Jesus.

As soon as Simeon saw Jesus, he took him in his arms and gave thanks to God. Then he said, 'Now O Lord, your servant may die in peace, for with my own eyes I have seen your salvation.'

Mary and Joseph were amazed to hear Simeon say these things about Jesus. Simeon blessed them and said to Mary, 'This child will save Israel. He will be a sign from God, but many people will speak against him and cause you much sorrow.'

Then a very old lady named Anna came up. She was a prophetess, and she spoke about Jesus to everyone who was hoping the Saviour would soon come.

Anna and Simeon realized that Jesus was the longed for Messiah.

An important event happened in Jesus' life when he was twelve years old. He was now old enough to go with Mary and Joseph to the Passover feast in Jerusalem.

When the feast was over, all the pilgrims set off to walk back home. They travelled in large parties for safety.

Mary and Joseph had been walking for a day when they realized that Jesus was not with their party. They had thought he was with some relatives and friends who were also on their way back but he was nowhere to be found.

'We'd better go back towards Jerusalem,' said Joseph who was very worried. He and Mary set off back to look for the boy. No one whom they met on the road had seen Jesus.

It was three days before they found him. He was in the temple, sitting with the Jewish teachers, listening to them and asking them questions. The teachers were amazed at his understanding and at all the wonderful things he said.

Mary said, 'Why did you stay behind like this? Your father and I have been very worried looking for you.'

Jesus looked up at them in surprise. He had expected them to go straight to the temple when they looked for him.

'Didn't you know that I was bound to be in my Father's house?' he asked. Mary and Joseph could not understand what he meant.

Jesus went back with them to Nazareth where he was obedient and helpful. He grew up to be strong and wise and everyone loved him.

The Baptism of Jesus

WHEN Zechariah's son, John, grew up, he knew that he must go out and tell people that the coming of the Messiah was very near.

John was a strange-looking man, and crowds of people came to hear him as he preached in the desert. He wore rough clothes made of camel's hair and had a leather belt round his waist. For food, he ate locusts and wild honey.

'Turn away from your sins!' he cried. 'Come and be baptized, repent and God will forgive you.'

Many people came from Jerusalem and from the country of Judea and around the River Jordan. They were sorry for their past sins, and John baptized them in the river as a sign that their sins were washed away and they had a new start in life.

Members of the main religious parties, the Pharisees and the Saducees, came too. Some of them were proud and thought they were better than other people.

'Who said you would escape punishment for your sins?' cried John sternly. 'You must do things which show you are sorry for your sins. It is the way you live now that matters. Good trees bear good fruit.'

'What must we do?' the people asked him.

'You should share your goods with people who are poorer than you are,' said John.

'What about us?' asked some tax-collectors standing nearby.

'Don't collect more money than is legal,' said John.

To some soldiers he said, 'Don't try to get money from other people by force. Be satisfied with your wages.'

Some of the people thought that John must be the longed-for Messiah, and they asked him if this was so.

'No,' replied John. 'I baptize you with water, to show you have repented of your sins. But there is one coming who is much greater than I, and I am not good enough even to unfasten his shoes. He will baptize you with the Holy Spirit.'

Not long after this, Jesus himself came to the River Jordan and asked John the Baptist to baptize him.

John protested. 'Surely *you* should baptize *me*!' he said.

Jesus replied that it was right for John to baptize him.

So John immersed Jesus in the water. As Jesus came up out of the water, John saw the heavens open and the spirit of God came down in the form of a dove. And a voice from heaven said,

'This is my beloved son with whom I am pleased.'

The Temptations

AFTER he had been baptized, Jesus was led by God's Holy Spirit into the wilderness. There he would be alone and he could have time to think and pray about his work. It was a lonely, empty desert place and he was there for forty days. During all that time he ate nothing and he became very hungry.

Then he heard the voice of the devil say to him, 'If you are God's son, you could make these stones turn into bread.'

Now Jesus knew that God's powers were not given to him to use for himself. He also knew that people do not only need food for their bodies. They also need truth to feed their souls, and that sort of food comes through listening to God and obeying his laws.

So he said to the devil, 'The scripture says that men cannot live on bread alone. They need God's word too.'

Then the devil tried again. This time he showed Jesus all the kingdoms of the world.

'All this,' said the devil, 'could be yours, if only you will worship me and follow my ways.'

Jesus knew that worshipping the devil meant living a life of evil words and deeds. Again he quoted the scripture, saying, 'You shall love the Lord your God, and you shall serve only him.'

Then the devil tried a third time. He suggested that Jesus should throw himself down from the highest part of the temple building. 'God's angels will take care of you,' he said. 'You won't hurt yourself at all.'

If Jesus had done this, no doubt lots of people would have flocked to him, thinking he was a magician, but Jesus knew that men must turn to God in their hearts. So he said,

'The scripture says, "You must not test the Lord God."'

The devil gave up and left Jesus alone in the wilderness.

Jesus calls his Disciples

WHEN Jesus began his work of preaching about God's good news, he chose some people to help him. They did not have to be rich or important or clever people – all they needed was a love of God and the right spirit to follow Jesus.

As Jesus walked by the Lake of Galilee one day, he saw the brothers Andrew and Peter, who were fishermen, at their work. They were using a net to catch fish in the lake.

Jesus said to them, 'Come with me and I will make you fishers of men.' Immediately they left their fishing and followed him.

A little further on he saw two more brothers, James and John. They were in a boat with their father. Jesus called them too, and they left their boat and followed him.

Another man whom Jesus chose was a tax-collector named Matthew. Most people thought tax-collectors were bad men, but Jesus looked for the good in men's hearts.

In all he chose twelve men who were to be especially close to him and who were to learn from him and help him in his work. These twelve were called apostles – a word which means 'people who are sent with a message'.

There were many other people who followed Jesus. His small group grew until a large number of people followed him. Some stayed with him all the time and gave up their jobs, while others returned to their homes and their work from time to time. All were disciples, which means learners. They learnt from the example of their teacher, Jesus.

The Fishermen's Catch

ONE day Jesus was on the shore by the lake. The crowds were pushing towards him to hear him speak. There were two empty boats at the water's edge, and stepping into one which belonged to Peter, he asked for it to be pushed out a little. Now he could sit in the boat and all the people would be able to see and hear him better.

When he had finished speaking, he said to Peter, 'Push the boat out further where the water is deeper, and when you let down your nets you will catch lots of fish.'

'Master,' said Peter, 'we've been working all through the night and have caught nothing. But we'll try again.'

They did so, and this time they caught so many fish that the nets were almost breaking. They had to ask their partners in the other boat to come and help them unload. Very soon both boats were so full of fish that they nearly sank. The fishermen were all amazed at this wonderful happening.

Peter knelt down before Jesus and said, 'Lord, please leave me! I am too great a sinner for you!'

'Don't be afraid,' said Jesus. 'From now on you will be catching people, not fish.'

The fishermen left their boats and their nets and followed Jesus, learning his ways and helping him to win men for God.

Water into Wine

ONE day there was a wedding in the village of Cana. Jesus had been invited and so had his mother, Mary, and his disciples.

In the middle of the wedding party, the supply of wine ran out, and the man who was in charge felt very embarrassed. He did not know what to do.

Mary noticed what had happened and she went and told Jesus. Then she went to the servants and said, 'Do whatever Jesus tells you.'

Jesus saw that there were six huge water jars standing nearby, each one big enough to hold about a hundred litres.

'Fill those up with water,' he said to the servants, and they did so.

'Now draw some out and take it to the man in charge,' he said.

Again the servants obeyed. The man in charge wondered what was happening, but he tasted the drink which the servants brought him – and instead of being water, it had been turned into wine!

He did not know where this wine had come from, so he called the bridegroom over to him and said,

'This is wonderful wine! You're different from most people. Usually they give guests the best wine first. Then if any more is needed, they use ordinary wine. But you have kept the best wine until the last!'

This was the first miracle Jesus had performed. When the disciples saw what had happened, they knew that Jesus really was the Messiah sent to bring joy to God's people.

Healing the Sick

PETER invited Jesus to the house where both he and his brother Andrew lived. When they arrived, they found that Peter's mother-in-law was very ill with a fever.

As soon as Jesus heard, he went to the sick mother, took hold of her hand and helped her up. The fever left her and she was able to help with a meal.

The news of this soon spread, and sick people were brought to Jesus wherever he went. Often they were carried to him by friends or relatives. Jesus placed his hands on them and they were cured.

A man who had been ill for thirty-eight years was made better at the word of Jesus. A crippled woman who had not been able to stand straight for eighteen years was cured when Jesus touched her.

Sometimes Jesus healed on the Sabbath day, which was the weekly day of rest. The authorities objected to Jesus healing anyone on that day as their laws said no work should be done on the Sabbath.

'Wouldn't you rescue an animal which had fallen into a pit on the Sabbath?' Jesus asked them. 'Isn't it right to do good and save life on the Sabbath?'

One day some people brought Jesus a man who was deaf and could not speak properly. Because he was deaf, he could not hear sounds to imitate. Jesus took him aside from the crowd, put his fingers in the man's ears and touched his tongue. Then he looked up to heaven. These were signs to the man that Jesus, with God's power, would heal him. 'Open,' said Jesus, and at once the man could hear and was able to speak properly.

Another man had a withered hand, and Jesus healed it so that it became just as normal as his other hand.

In those days people were frightened of catching a dreadful skin disease called leprosy. It was believed that leprosy was a punishment from God for sinners. Lepers were thought to be unclean and they had to live far away from everyone else but Jesus often went near them. Whether people were sick or poor or weak or helpless, Jesus was their friend.

Once, as he was going to Jerusalem, he was met by ten men who were lepers. They stood at a distance, for they were not used to anyone coming close to them, and they shouted, 'Jesus! Master! Make us well!'

Jesus came up to them and said simply, 'Go and show yourselves to the priests.'

This had to be done before they were allowed to go back among other people. The men set off, and as they were going, they saw that their terrible sores had disappeared. Their leprosy was cured. How delighted they were! One of the ten, who was a Samaritan, went back to Jesus to say thank you. He bowed low at Jesus' feet and shouted out his praises to God.

'But where are the other nine?' asked Jesus. 'Didn't I make ten men well?'

The nine, like many other people, had forgotten to thank God for his goodness to them.

Jesus heals a Paralysed Man

IN Capernaum there was a man who had an illness called palsy. He could not get up and walk like other people.

Day after day he lay at home. He worried about all the sinful things he had done which had probably brought on his illness. Fortunately he had four kind friends and they used to come and tell him all the news.

One day they said to him, 'Jesus the teacher is back in Capernaum. There are crowds following him everywhere, and he has made lots of sick people better.'

'If only I could get to him,' sighed the paralysed man, 'perhaps he could cure me too. But there is no hope of that for I can't walk, and he isn't likely to come to this house.'

Then one of the friends had an idea. 'Why couldn't we take you to him?' he suggested. 'We could carry you on your bed.'

'We know the house where Jesus is teaching,' said another. 'Come on, we'll take you there now!'

The paralysed man had no time to argue. The friends each picked up a corner of his mattress, and they carried him off down the street, straight to the house where Jesus was.

When they got there, they found they could not get in. There were so many people listening to Jesus that the house was filled with people. They were even jammed in the doorway, and crowding round in the street outside. The four friends could not get near Jesus, and the sick man was terribly disappointed. Now he would never see Jesus, he thought.

His friends, however, were not going to be put off so easily. They were sure Jesus would help if they could only reach him.

The house had a flat roof and an outside staircase leading up to it – like many houses in that part of the world. This gave the friends another idea. They struggled up the staircase, carrying the man on his bed, and went out on to the flat roof. Then they made an opening in the roof, just above the place where Jesus was standing.

The crowd inside felt air blowing on them from above. They looked up and, to their great surprise, saw the man being lowered gently down by ropes on his mattress, until he landed right in front of Jesus.

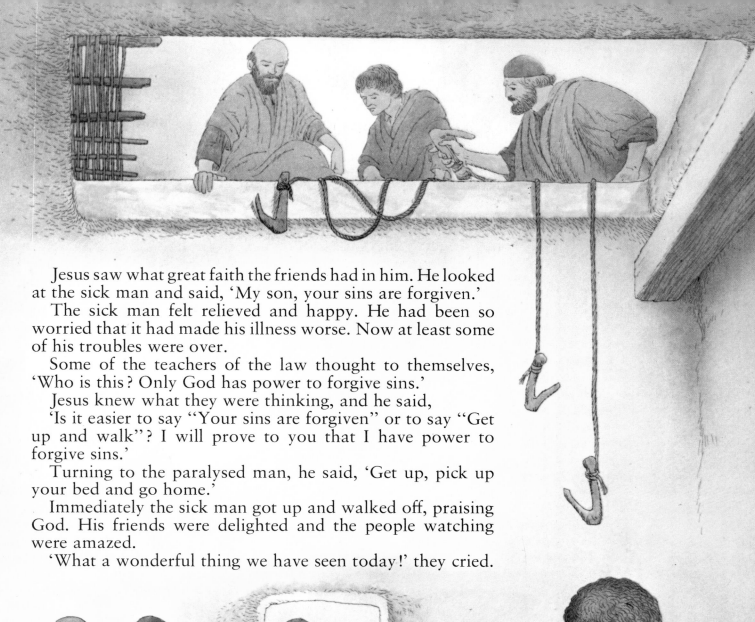

Jesus saw what great faith the friends had in him. He looked at the sick man and said, 'My son, your sins are forgiven.'

The sick man felt relieved and happy. He had been so worried that it had made his illness worse. Now at least some of his troubles were over.

Some of the teachers of the law thought to themselves, 'Who is this? Only God has power to forgive sins.'

Jesus knew what they were thinking, and he said,

'Is it easier to say "Your sins are forgiven" or to say "Get up and walk"? I will prove to you that I have power to forgive sins.'

Turning to the paralysed man, he said, 'Get up, pick up your bed and go home.'

Immediately the sick man got up and walked off, praising God. His friends were delighted and the people watching were amazed.

'What a wonderful thing we have seen today!' they cried.

Jairus' Daughter

BY the lakeside a great crowd was listening to Jesus. Suddenly a man came hurrying up and knelt at Jesus' feet. His name was Jairus and he was an official of the synagogue.

'My daughter is very sick – she is dying! She is only twelve. Please come and make her better!' he begged Jesus.

'I will come,' said Jesus, and he started to go with Jairus to his home. The disciples and many of the crowd followed.

In the crowd was a woman who had been ill for twelve years with bad bleeding. She had spent all her money on doctors, but they had not been able to make her better. She had heard about Jesus, and she said to herself,

'If only I touch the hem of his cloak, I shall get well again.'

So she pushed her way through the crowd, bent down, and touched the hem. Her bleeding stopped at once.

'Who touched me?' asked Jesus.

'Master,' said the disciples, 'the people are crowding all round you, and yet you ask "Who touched me?".'

Jesus said, 'I know someone touched me, for power went out from me.'

Trembling, the woman threw herself down at Jesus' feet. She told him why she had touched him, and that now she was healed.

Jesus looked at her kindly and said,

'Your faith in me has made you well. Go in peace.'

While he was saying this, a messenger from Jairus' home came running up.

'Don't bother the master any more,' he said sadly, 'for your little daughter has died.'

Jesus turned to Jairus and said, 'Don't be afraid. Just go on believing and she will be well.'

He continued the journey as though the messenger had never come. When they reached Jairus' house, everyone was crying and the musicians were getting ready for the child's funeral. Jesus asked them all to stay outside except his three disciples, Peter, James and John, who went indoors with him.

'Don't cry,' said Jesus to the family. 'The child is not dead – she is only sleeping.'

The people laughed at this, and Jesus took Jairus and his wife and the three disciples into the room where the child was lying. He went up to the bed, took the girl by the hand and said,

'Get up, child!' and the little girl's life came back to her at once. She got up, and Jesus asked the astounded parents to give her something to eat.

Feeding the Five Thousand

PEOPLE flocked around Jesus, and on some days he was so busy teaching and healing them that he hardly had time to eat.

On one of these busy days, Jesus felt that he and his disciples needed some time to be alone and rest. So they started out in a boat to row across to the other side of the lake.

Many people, however, saw them leave, and they followed them round by the land. Some even ran ahead and reached the other side of the lake before the boat.

Jesus got out of the boat and saw the large crowd. There were other people still climbing the hills looking for him, and he felt sorry for them. They seemed like sheep without a shepherd. He welcomed them and continued to teach and heal them. There were about five thousand men there, and many women and children.

In the evening, the disciples came to him and said,

'It is very late, and this is a lonely place. The people are getting hungry. Why not send them away so that they can go to the farms and villages and buy themselves something to eat?'

Jesus asked, 'Where can we buy bread to feed all these people?'

'It would cost a fortune,' said Philip, one of the disciples.

Then Andrew came up and said,

'There is a lad here who has brought five barley loaves and two fish with him – but that won't be enough to feed this crowd.'

'Tell everyone to sit down,' ordered Jesus. 'Divide them into groups of about fifty in each group.'

The people sat down on the grass. They looked very colourful in their bright robes.

Jesus took the loaves and the fish which the boy offered him and, looking upwards, he gave thanks to God. Then he broke the loaves and gave them to the disciples to hand round to the people. He also divided the fish among the vast crowd and everyone had enough to eat.

'Now gather up the scraps that are left,' said Jesus to the disciples, 'We must not waste anything.'

The disciples went round collecting, and were able to fill twelve baskets with the pieces left over.

When the people realized that Jesus had performed another miracle, they said, 'Surely this man must be the prophet we have all been expecting!'

Jesus' Power on the Water

ONE evening, Jesus and his disciples were in a boat on the lake. Suddenly, a fierce wind blew up and great waves began to splash over their little boat. It was in danger of sinking.

The disciples were terrified – more so when they found that Jesus was asleep in the back of the boat. They hurried to him and woke him up.

'Master! Master! Save us!' they cried. 'We shall all be drowned!'

Jesus answered calmly, 'Why are you so afraid? Where is your faith?'

Then he got up and said to the wind, 'Be quiet' and to the waves, 'Be still!'

The wind died down and the waves became peaceful and calm.

The disciples were amazed and still rather frightened. They said to each other, 'Who is this man? Even the winds and the waves obey him!'

Another time the disciples were in a boat by themselves. It was a windy evening, and the boat, far out into the lake, was being tossed by the waves.

It grew dark. They had rowed 5 or 6 kilometres when they saw a figure walking towards them across the water.

'It's a ghost!' they screamed.

It was not a ghost. It was Jesus and he said to them, 'Courage! It is I. Don't be afraid!'

Then Peter said, 'If it is really you, Lord, order me to walk on the water to you.'

'Come,' said Jesus, and Peter got out of the boat and started to walk on the water to Jesus. Suddenly his courage failed and he began to sink. Jesus reached out and seized him and they both got safely into the boat.

'How little faith you have!' said Jesus. 'Why did you have any doubts?'

The other disciples were astonished, and they said, 'Truly, you are the Son of God!'

The Lord's Prayer

THE disciples noticed that Jesus often prayed, so they asked him about prayer.

Jesus said they should not pray in a place where everyone could see them, for prayer was not something to show off about.

'Go to your room and close the door,' said Jesus. 'Your father, God, will hear you and see you, and that is what matters. There is no need to use a lot of long words. Some people think that God will hear them because of their long words, but God hears short, simple prayers just as well.

'Ask God for what you need, just as you would ask a good father. If it is good for you to have it, then God will give it to you. If he does not give it to you, then it is because he knows it is better that you should not have it.'

One of the disciples said, 'Lord, teach us to pray.'

Jesus gave them a pattern prayer which has been used ever since. It is called *The Lord's Prayer*.

'Our Father in heaven:
May your holy name be honoured;
may your Kingdom come;
may your will be done on earth as it is in heaven.
Give us today the food we need.
Forgive us the wrongs we have done, as we forgive the
  wrongs that others have done to us.
Do not bring us to hard testing, but keep us safe
  from the Evil One.'

The Prodigal Son

ALL sorts of people came to listen to Jesus. He often told them parables. The parables were stories stories about everyday life which taught lessons about God.

Jesus never turned anyone away, no matter who they were. Outcasts were just as welcome as the most important members of society.

This made the Pharisees and teachers of the law grumble. 'Jesus even welcomes sinners and eats with them,' they said.

Jesus knew what they thought so one day he told this parable.

There was once a man who had two sons. They knew that when their father died, his money and goods would be divided between them. The younger one could not wait. He said to his father,

'Father, give me my share of the property now.'

So the father agreed and the younger son sold his share, took the money and left home.

He went away to a far country, and began to waste his money in silly and selfish ways. It was not long before he found he had none left. Then a severe famine came to that country and the son did not know how he would survive. At last he took a job, looking after pigs.

As he watched the pigs feeding, he began to think seriously.

'How I wish I had even the food the pigs eat,' he sighed. 'My father's servants have more than enough to eat, and here am I, his son, starving! I will go back to my father, and tell him that I have sinned against God and against him, and I'll ask him to treat me as one of his servants.'

So, he got up and started on the long journey back home, wondering how his father would receive him. He was still a long way from home, when his father saw him coming and ran out to meet him. He threw his arms round his son's neck and kissed him, for he had been hoping for the boy's return for a very long time.

Then the son said humbly, 'Father, I have sinned against God and against you. I am not fit to be called your son.'

His father did not seem to be listening. 'Bring out the best robe,' he called to his servants. 'Put a ring on his finger, and shoes on his feet. Kill the calf that has been fattened for a special occasion, for we must have a feast to celebrate. This son, whom we thought was lost, has now been found. We thought he was dead, but he is alive!'

The entire household began to rejoice and make merry, all except the older brother. He was working in the fields when his brother came home, and when he heard about the feast, he was jealous and angry and refused to join in.

'My son,' said the father, 'you are always with me, and all I have is yours. But now your brother is sorry he went away and he has returned home so we must celebrate.'

The Lost Sheep

JESUS often saw shepherds and their sheep as he went about the countryside. In Eastern countries, the shepherd did not drive his sheep, he led them. They would follow him as he took them to fresh pastures and to water, and they knew he would not leave them.

A shepherd's life was a dangerous one, for he had to be ready to fight off any wild animals which came prowling after his flock, or any robbers who came to steal the sheep. He was ready to give his life for his sheep. If he had to take them through mountainous and rocky country, he was always ready to protect them from falling by using his staff.

He knew all his sheep by name, and the sheep knew his voice and followed him. They would never follow if a stranger called to them. If one of his flock strayed and was missing, the shepherd would search high and low until he found it.

At night-time, when he had led the flock safely into the sheepfold, he would lie across the doorway himself, so that none of his sheep could wander out, and no wild animal could get in. He was the door of the sheepfold.

One day Jesus told a story about a shepherd.

Suppose a man has one hundred sheep, and one of them wanders away and is lost. He does not forget about it and say to himself, 'I still have ninety-nine others'.

He leaves the ninety-nine grazing safely, while he goes and searches until he finds the lost one. When he finds it, he is very happy. He picks it up and carries it home on his shoulders.

Then he calls together his friends and neighbours and says, 'Come and celebrate with me! I have found the sheep which I had lost!'

'In just the same way,' Jesus continued, 'there is rejoicing in heaven when someone who has strayed and done wrong comes back to God.'

Another time, Jesus said, 'I know my sheep and they know me. If a hired man, who is not the shepherd, sees a wolf coming, he deserts the sheep and runs away. But I am the good shepherd who is willing to die for his sheep.'

The Talents

JESUS once told this story to show that people should make the most of the skills and abilities which God has given them.

There was a nobleman who had to go away on a long journey to a far country. Before he left, he called his servants together and put them in charge of his property. He gave them each as much as he thought they would be able to manage. To the first servant he gave five talents (a talent was a large amount of money). He gave two talents to the second servant and to the third he gave one talent.

After he had gone, the first two servants took their money and traded with it wisely, so that the amount of the money doubled. The third servant just dug a deep hole and buried his money. It was no use at all in the ground.

The nobleman was away a long time, and when he came back, he called his servants together to find out what they had been doing.

The first servant said, 'Sir, you gave me five talents. I traded with them and they have earned another five.'

'Well done, good and faithful servant!' said his master. 'You have been wise with this money. Now I will give you more to look after. Come and share my joy!'

The second servant said, 'Sir, I have earned another two talents with the two which you gave me.'

'Well done, good and faithful servant!' said the master. 'I will give you more money to manage. Come and share my joy!'

Then the third servant came up and said, 'Sir, I know you are a hard man who expects a lot, and I was afraid. So I hid your money in the ground. Look! Here it is.'

'You are a bad and lazy servant,' said the nobleman. 'At least you could have put my money in the bank where it would have earned some interest. I shall take the money from you, and give it to the servant who had the five talents. The man who uses what he has well, will gain more. The man who does not use his gifts, even if they are only small, will soon lose all that he has.'

The Sower

MANY people worked in the fields in Jesus' day. Jesus would often see a farmer walking up and down his field, throwing out handfuls of seed as he went. The fields were not ploughed before the seeds were scattered and the farmer knew that it was important for the seed to fall on land where it would grow.

Once when a big crowd had gathered round Jesus at the lakeside, he told them this story.

A man went out to sow his seed, but not all of it dropped where he intended it. Some of it fell on the path, where the ground had become hard with people walking on it. The birds soon flew down and ate up that seed.

Other seeds fell on rocky ground, where there was very little soil. These seeds began to sprout, but the roots could not grow deeply enough and there was not enough moisture. When the sun came out, it dried up the little plants so that they withered and died.

Some of the seed fell among thorns, and the thorns grew up with the little plants and choked them, and they too, died.

Some of the seed, however, fell on good soil, as the sower had wanted. These plants grew up and produced much new grain. Some had thirty grains, some sixty and some one hundred.

Later that day, when Jesus was alone, the disciples who had been listening came and asked him what the story meant. They knew that many of Jesus' stories were parables, and that parables teach a special lesson.

Jesus explained the story.

The seed is God's word, his message. The seeds that fell on the path are like the people who hear God's word but do not let it sink into their minds. Then the devil comes along and takes it away from them and urges them to think about other things. So they forget about God and the seed does not have a chance to grow.

The seeds that fall on rocky ground are like the people who hear God's message and accept it gladly at first. When troubles come, they give up at once, for the message is not deeply rooted in their hearts. Their thoughts of God are shallow, just as the soil on the rocky ground was shallow.

The seeds that fell in the thorns are like those people who start to live by God's word. Then they let other interests, worries and pleasures crowd it out of their lives. They no longer have time for God's word and so it becomes choked, and dies.

The seeds falling on good soil are very different. They are like the people who hear God's word and let it grow deeply in their hearts.

The Good Samaritan

ONE day a lawyer asked Jesus what he must do to gain everlasting life in heaven. Jesus asked him what the Jewish religious law said. The lawyer replied that he must love God with his heart, soul and strength, and that he must love his neighbour as he loved himself.

Then the lawyer wanted to know who was his neighbour. In reply, Jesus told this story.

A traveller was walking along the lonely, rocky road from Jerusalem to Jericho. Suddenly a band of robbers sprang out, and attacked and robbed him. They beat him up, tore off his clothes, and left him by the roadside half dead.

Soon afterwards a priest passed down the road. He saw the wounded man, but he walked past him on the other side.

A little later a Levite (an assistant at the temple) also came along. He crossed the road, looked at the man, and then walked by on the other side.

Next a Samaritan came along. He was not even from the wounded man's country, and normally the Jews and the Samaritans were not at all friendly towards one another.

When the Samaritan saw the wounded man, he felt very sorry for him. He got off his donkey and went over to see what he could do to help. When he saw how badly injured the man was, he used oil and wine to clean his wounds. Then he bandaged them up and made the man as comfortable as he could.

He put the man on his own donkey, while he himself walked beside it, and he took him to an inn. There he cared for the man, as though he had been his own brother.

Next day he had to leave the inn, so he gave the inn-keeper two silver coins and said,

'Please look after him. If you find this money is not enough, I will repay you any more you spend when I come back this way.'

'Now,' said Jesus to the lawyer, 'which of the three men who came along the road was neighbour to the man who was robbed?'

The lawyer replied, 'The one who was kind to him.'

'Then you go and do the same,' said Jesus.

The lawyer went thoughtfully away. Now he knew not only what the law said but also what it meant. He knew he must love his neighbour, but that his neighbour meant everyone he met every day. To be a real neighbour, he had to be prepared to show love and kindness even to those he thought of as his enemies.

The Kingdom of Heaven

J ESUS often talked about God's kingdom, the kingdom of heaven. The people listening to Jesus did not find it easy to understand as it was not like an earthly kingdom. So Jesus told them several little stories to show what he meant.

The kingdom of heaven, he said, is like a tiny mustard seed. Though mustard is the smallest of seeds, it grows into a huge plant – so big that the birds come and make their nests in its branches. The followers of Jesus began as a group of twelve ordinary men. From such a small beginning their faith has spread throughout the world. It goes on spreading, through the work of churches, schools and hospitals, through missionaries and teachers, and through the influence of ordinary people who believe in God.

The kingdom of heaven is also like yeast which is mixed with flour to make bread. It cannot be seen in the bread but it bubbles and swells and makes the dough rise. The kingdom of heaven spreads because God's spirit is working within people. 'The kingdom of heaven,' said Jesus, 'is within you.'

The kingdom of heaven is like treasure hidden in a field. When a man stumbles on it, he is so happy that he sells everything else he has in order to buy the field. The kingdom of heaven is also like a man searching for pearls. As soon as he finds the most beautiful one of all, he sells all he has in order to buy it. When people find God's way, whether by accident or whether they search for a long time, they gladly give up other things in order to serve him.

The kingdom of heaven is also like a net which the fishermen throw into the sea to catch all kinds of fish. When the net is full, they sort out the good from the bad. Everyone has the chance to be gathered into God's kingdom.

Lazarus

AT Bethany, Jesus had some good friends – Martha and Mary and their brother Lazarus.

One day Lazarus became seriously ill, and his sisters sent a message to Jesus for help.

Jesus said to his disciples, 'Our friend Lazarus is sleeping, but I will go and waken him.' The disciples did not at first understand that Jesus meant that Lazarus was already dead.

When they arrived at Bethany, they found that Lazarus had died and that he had been buried four days before. Many friends were comforting Martha and Mary on their brother's death. Martha came up to Jesus and said, 'Lord, if you had been here, Lazarus would not have died – but I know, even now, that God will grant whatever you ask.'

'Your brother will rise again!' said Jesus. 'Whoever believes in me will live again, even though he dies now. Do you believe that, Martha?'

'Yes, Lord,' replied Martha. 'I believe you are the Messiah.'

Then she went indoors and called Mary to come out. When Mary saw Jesus, she fell at his feet and wept.

'Where have you laid Lazarus?' Jesus asked.

'Come and see,' they answered, and they took Jesus to Lazarus' tomb which was a cave with a large stone in front.

'Take the stone away,' Jesus ordered.

They rolled away the big stone and Jesus prayed to God. Then he called out in a loud voice,

'Lazarus, come out!'

Lazarus came out of the tomb, still bound up in cloths and bandages.

'Unbind him and let him go,' commanded Jesus.

What great rejoicing there was at Bethany! Many of those who saw the miracle believed in Jesus, but there were others who went and reported him to the authorities.

'Soon everyone will believe in him,' they said, and they began to plot how they might get rid of him.

The Transfiguration

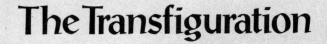

THERE was one occasion when Jesus took his three closest disciples up into a mountain with him. Jesus knelt down to pray and the three disciples noticed a great change come over him. His face became bright as the sun, and his clothes were a dazzling white. It was a glimpse of glory, and it is called the transfiguration.

Then they saw that Jesus was not alone. Two other figures were with him. One was Moses, the great leader of old, and the other was the mighty prophet Elijah. The disciples were frightened and hardly knew what to say. Peter wanted to make three tents there, one for Jesus, one for Moses, and one for Elijah.

While he was talking a cloud came down and covered them and a voice said, 'This is my beloved son. Listen to him.'

The disciples were terrified and threw themselves to the ground. Then Jesus came and touched them and said,

'Get up. Don't be frightened.'

They looked up and saw only Jesus was there.

When, a little later, they came down the mountain, they found a crowd of people arguing with the other disciples.

'What are you arguing about?' asked Jesus.

A man came through the crowd and knelt before Jesus.

'Sir, have pity on my son,' he said. 'He has an evil spirit and cannot talk. He has terrible fits and often falls into the fire or into water. I brought him to your disciples, but they could not heal him. Help me if you possibly can.'

'Everything is possible if you have faith,' said Jesus.

'I have faith,' said the man, 'but I don't have enough. Please help me to have more!'

'Bring the boy to me!' commanded Jesus.

They did so, and then Jesus said,

'Evil spirit, come out of this boy!'

The boy fell down and the people thought he was dead. Jesus took his hand and helped him up and then handed him to his father. He was cured.

Later the disciples asked Jesus privately, 'Why could we not heal the boy of the evil spirit?'

'You hadn't enough faith,' said Jesus. 'Only prayer can drive out evil like that.'

Zacchaeus

IN Jerico there lived a chief tax collector named Zacchaeus. No one liked tax collectors, for often they took more money than they were supposed to and kept it for themselves.

Zacchaeus was a very rich man, and he was also quite small. When Jesus came to Jericho, Zacchaeus wanted to see him but the crowd was so large that poor Zacchaeus could not see over their heads. Then he had an idea.

'I'll climb a tree,' he thought. 'I'll be sure to see then.'

He ran ahead of the crowd and climbed up into a sycamore tree. Now he was higher than anyone else and could see easily. He was pleased he had had such a good idea.

Along came Jesus and the crowd, and suddenly, to Zacchaeus' surprise, Jesus looked right up into the tree and saw him!

'Hurry down, Zacchaeus,' he said, 'for I'm coming to your house.'

Zacchaeus was astonished but he scrambled down from the tree and rushed home so that he could welcome Jesus.

Some of the people watching started to grumble.

'What's this? Jesus has gone to be a guest in the home of a man who is a sinner.'

Meanwhile Jesus had arrived at Zacchaeus' house. When Jesus looked at him, Zacchaeus knew how wrong he had been in the past to take more taxes than he should. He decided there and then to change his ways.

He said to Jesus, 'I will give half of all my belongings to the poor, and if I have cheated anyone in the past, I will pay him back four times as much as I took from him.'

'You have been saved today,' said Jesus. 'I came to seek and to save those who had lost the right way to live.'

Palm Sunday

JESUS and his disciples were on their way to Jerusalem for the feast of the Passover. The city was crowded with visitors. Many of them were hoping to see Jesus, because they had heard of the wonderful things he had done. However some of the chief priests and Pharisees were hoping to take him prisoner. They did not approve of his teachings and were jealous that so many people followed him.

The disciples were rather troubled on this journey to Jerusalem, for Jesus looked so solemn.

He took them aside and said, 'We're going up to Jerusalem where the Son of Man will be condemned to death. After three days he will be raised to life again.' He was talking about himself.

The disciples were puzzled and alarmed, but they walked on until they came to Bethphage by the Mount of Olives. Jesus called two of his disciples and said to them,

'Go to the village that lies ahead. As soon as you enter you will find a donkey tied up which has never been ridden. Untie it and bring it here. If anyone asks what you are doing, you are to say, "The Lord needs it and will send it back here." Then they will let you bring it.'

Everything happened just as Jesus had said. Jesus had chosen to ride a donkey because it was looked on as a symbol of peace whereas the horse was a symbol of pride and war. He wanted to show the kind of king he was – not a warrior king who had come to conquer by force, but a peaceful king whose rule was the rule of love.

When the two disciples brought the animal back, they threw their cloaks over it and Jesus rode it into Jerusalem. When the crowds saw him coming, they spread their cloaks on the roadway, as they would do for a king. Others cut branches from the trees and spread them on the road. Everybody shouted and cheered.

Jesus was now in the centre of a great crowd, some going ahead, some following behind, and some who had come out from Jerusalem to meet him. They were waving palm branches and shouting, 'Hosanna! Praise to God! God bless him who comes in the name of the Lord!'

Some people did not know why there was such an uproar. 'Who is this?' they asked.

The crowds told them, 'This is Jesus, the prophet from Nazareth in Galilee.'

Some of the Pharisees in the city feared trouble if the crowd was heard shouting and cheering a king other than Caesar. They went up to Jesus and said, 'Make your followers be quiet!'

Jesus would not. 'If they were quiet, the stones on the road would cry out,' he said.

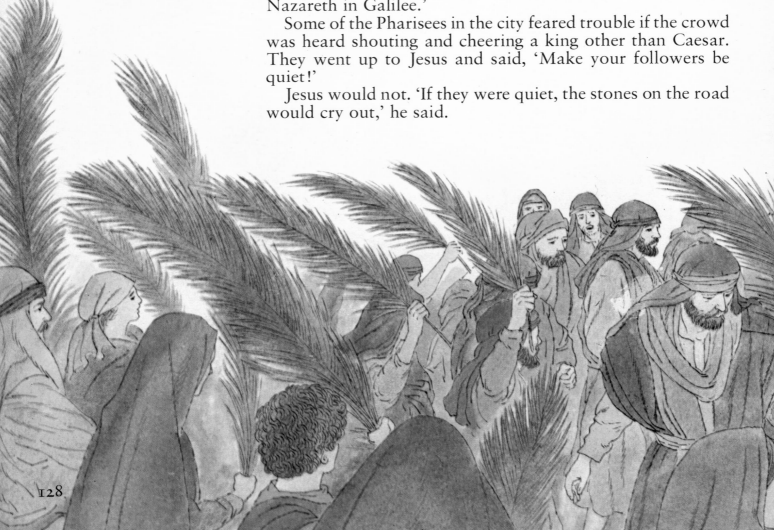

When he saw Jerusalem stretched out before him, his eyes filled with tears. He was sad that such a lovely city had so many people in it who were full of hatred and wickedness.

The next day Jesus went into the temple and found the moneychangers who were changing foreign money into Jewish money. This was so that people could pay taxes or buy animals for sacrifice. These men were dealing dishonestly and cheating people.

Jesus was very angry at this shameful behaviour, especially in God's house. So he overturned the tables of the deceitful moneychangers and the seats of those who sold pigeons for sacrifice. He drove them out and said, 'It is written in the scriptures that God said, "My house shall be called a house of prayer" – but you are making it a den of thieves.'

The Last Supper

'WHERE do you want us to get the Passover meal ready?' asked the disciples of Jesus.

It was the Thursday after Jesus' entry into Jerusalem and Jesus knew that this would be his last night on earth, before returning to God his Father.

'Go into the city,' he said, 'and there you will see a man carrying a jar of water. Follow him, and when he goes into a house, go to the owner of the house and say, "Where is the room where the Master and his disciples will eat the Passover?" Then he will show you an upstairs room.'

The disciples went and found everything as Jesus had said. It was easy to find the man with the water jar, because it was the women who usually carried the stone water jars.

That evening, Jesus and the twelve disciples sat together for the meal. It was usual before a meal for a servant to wash the feet of the guests – a welcome service in a hot, dusty land. This time, Jesus himself took a towel and began to wash the feet of the disciples. He, the greatest among them all, did the work of a servant.

After he had washed their feet, Jesus sat down and said, 'Do you understand what I have just been doing? You call me Master and Lord, and that is true. If I, your Master and

Lord, have washed your feet, then you should also wash one another's feet. I have set an example for you to follow.'

The disciples began to understand that no one is too great to serve others.

As they were eating, Jesus said, 'One of you will betray me.'

The disciples were puzzled and upset and asked whom he meant.

Jesus said, 'It is the one who dips his bread in the dish with me. It would be better if he had never been born.'

Then the disciples saw Judas Iscariot dipping his bread in the dish.

Jesus said to the disciples, 'Love one another, as I have loved you. Then people will know that you are my disciples.'

He took a piece of bread, gave a prayer of thanks, broke it, and shared it with the disciples. 'Take and eat this,' he said, 'for this is my body.'

Then he took a cup, gave thanks to God, and passed it round, saying, 'Drink this, for this is my blood shed for many.'

It was a meal the disciples would never forget. They finished the meal, sang a Passover psalm together, and went out to the Mount of Olives.

The Garden of Gethsemane

'TONIGHT, you will all run away and leave me,' said Jesus to his disciples.

'Never!' said Peter. 'Even if the rest do, I won't!'

Jesus looked at Peter and said, 'Before the cock crows twice tonight, you will have said three times that you do not know me.'

They went into a garden called Gethsemane and Jesus said to them, 'Sit here while I go and pray over there.' He went ahead, taking only Peter, James and John with him.

'The sorrow in my heart is very great,' Jesus said. 'Stay here and watch.' He went a little further alone.

There he threw himself on the ground and prayed to God.

'Father, if it is possible, take this suffering away from me. Yet I know it's not my will, but your will that must be done.'

Then he went back to the three disciples and found they had fallen asleep. They were very weary and that evening they fell asleep three times while Jesus was praying. After the third time, Jesus said,

'The time has come for the Son of Man to be handed over to wicked men. Get up, for here comes the man who is going to betray me.'

The disciples turned and saw a crowd of soldiers sent by the chief priests of the temple approaching through the trees. They were carrying swords and clubs, and with them was Judas Iscariot, one of Jesus' disciples. The soldiers were not sure which man they had been ordered to arrest, but Judas said to them,

'The man I kiss is the one you want.' For this betrayal they agreed to pay Judas thirty pieces of silver.

Judas came up to Jesus saying 'Hail, Master!' and kissed him. Immediately the soldiers seized Jesus. Peter was so angry that he took his sword and cut off the ear of the high priest's servant, but Jesus immediately healed it.

The disciples were so terrified that they all ran away and left Jesus. Then the soldiers bound him and took him to the

house of Caiaphas, the high priest. The chief priests and teachers of the law had also gathered there. They tried their hardest to find some false evidence against Jesus so that they could have him put to death, but they could find nothing. At last they asked, 'Tell us if you are the Messiah, the Son of God?'

When Jesus said he was, Caiaphas was furious.

'Blasphemy!' he shouted. 'We don't need any more witnesses. You have heard his wicked words. What is your decision?'

'He is guilty and must be put to death,' shouted the others.

Now Peter, although he had run away with the others, wanted to find out what was happening to his master. So he came back and followed behind the crowd at a safe distance. When he reached the high priest's house, he went into the courtyard and warmed himself by the fire which had been lit there.

A servant girl passed by and said, 'Aren't you one of that man's disciples?'

'No,' said Peter. 'I don't know who you are talking about.'

Then someone else said, 'He was with Jesus of Nazareth.'

Again Peter denied it, saying, 'I swear I do not know him.'

After a little while a man standing near said, 'You are from Galilee. I can tell by the way you speak. You must be one of them.'

'I tell you I don't know the man,' insisted Peter.

Just then a cock crowed, and Peter remembered that Jesus had said he would deny him three times before the cock crowed. Peter wept bitterly.

The Crucifixion

THE chief priests did not have the power to put Jesus to death, so they sent him, bound in chains, to the Roman governor, Pontius Pilate.

'We want this man crucified,' demanded the chief priests. Pilate did not want to do this, especially as his wife had had a dream about Jesus, and had sent him a message saying, 'Do no harm to this just man.'

At every Passover feast it was the custom for the people to choose one prisoner to be set free. When Pilate asked the crowd which prisoner they wanted to be released, he hoped that they would say Jesus.

Earlier the chief priests had been among the crowd telling them to ask for Barabbas, a bandit and a murderer, so when Pilate put his question, they all shouted, 'Barabbas! Barabbas!'

Pilate saw it was useless to try and persuade the people to change their minds, so he sent for a bowl of water and washed his hands in front of the people to show that he was not responsible for Jesus' death. Then he released Barabbas. He ordered his men to whip Jesus.

Then the soldiers made a crown of thorns for him, and mocked him. 'Hail, King of the Jews!' they shouted.

They took him to be crucified on a hill called Calvary, outside Jerusalem. There they nailed him to the cross between two thieves who were also to be crucified. Over Jesus' head, Pilate wrote a notice saying, 'Jesus of Nazareth, King of the Jews.'

The soldiers divided Jesus' clothes among them and threw dice to see who should have his seamless robe.

Jesus looked down from the cross at the crowd. 'He saves others but he can't save himself,' they mocked. Then Jesus prayed, 'Father, forgive them for they don't know what they are doing.'

Then one of the two thieves said, 'Lord, remember me when you reign in your kingdom.'

'Today you will be with me in paradise,' Jesus replied, for this thief was sorry for his sins.

Although it was only the middle of the day, it suddenly grew dark over all the land. The darkness lasted for three hours.

'My God! My God! Why have you forsaken me?' cried Jesus. When he called, 'I am thirsty', someone dipped a sponge in wine and held it up to him.

Then Jesus said, 'It is finished!' A little later he said in prayer, 'Father, into your hands I give my spirit.' Then he died.

At that moment there was a great earthquake, and the curtain which hung in the temple before the Most Holy Place was split in two. The soldiers were terrified at these happenings, but the Roman centurion looking on realized who Jesus was. 'This man really was the Son of God!'

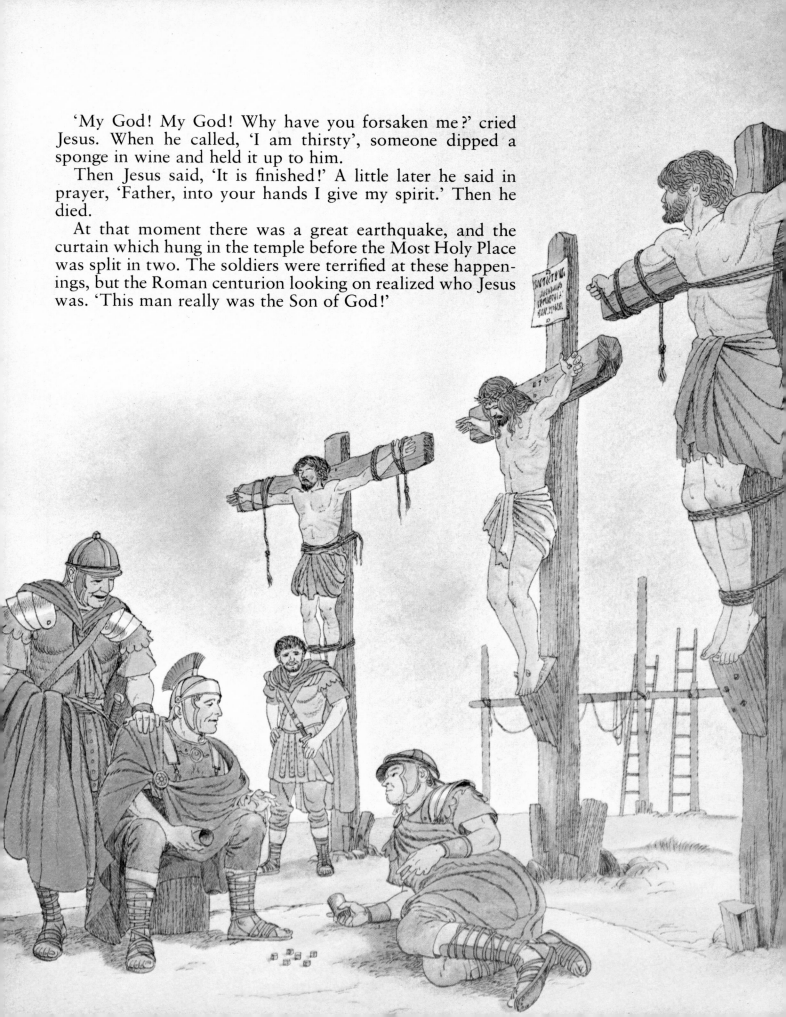

That evening a man named Joseph of Arimathea, who was a follower of Jesus, asked Pilate if he could take Jesus' body and put it in the tomb that he had had carved out of rock for his own body. Pilate agreed, so Joseph took the body, wrapped it in linen, and placed it in the cave-like tomb. A large stone was rolled across the entrance.

Mary Magdalene and her friends saw where the body was laid. They did not have time to anoint it with the usual sweet-smelling spices because it was the evening of the Sabbath and the law said they were to rest on the Sabbath.

Some of the chief priests and Pharisees remembered that Jesus had said he would rise to life again after three days. So they went to Pilate and asked,

'Will you have the grave guarded in case the disciples come and steal the body and then try to pretend Jesus has risen?'

'You have a guard of soldiers,' said Pilate. 'Go and make it as secure as you can.'

So the soldiers went and sealed the tomb.

The First Easter Morning

EARLY on the Sunday morning after the crucifixion, Mary Magdalene and her friends went to Jesus' tomb to take the spices to anoint Jesus' body.

As they made their way to the tomb, a dreadful thought struck them.

'How shall we get into the tomb?' they asked one another. 'There is a great stone closing the entrance – far too big for us to move.'

They walked on, hoping perhaps that they would find someone to help them. At last, they arrived at the tomb.

'Look!' said Mary. 'The stone has been moved!'

They gazed at it in astonishment. Then they went nearer the tomb until they could see inside. The body of Jesus was no longer there! They wondered what could have happened.

While they were puzzling about it, two angels in shining robes appeared. The women were frightened and bowed low, and the angels said, 'Why are you looking in a tomb for someone who is alive? Jesus is not here. He has risen from the dead. Don't you remember what he told you in Galilee – that he would be crucified by evil men, but that he would rise again on the third day? He is going to Galilee. You will see him there!'

Then they remembered that Jesus had indeed said these things, but at the time they had not understood him.

Scarcely knowing what to do, the women turned back and hurried to the place where Jesus' disciples had gathered. They burst in on the sad disciples with the amazing news.

The disciples found it too much to believe. 'Nonsense!' they said, 'It can't be true. You're making it up!'

Peter and John decided to go to the tomb to find out for themselves. They ran off, as fast as they could, and John, being the younger, got there first. He stooped down and looked in the cave, but he did not go inside. When Peter caught up, he rushed right past John and saw the linen clothes which had been wrapped round Jesus' body.

John followed into the tomb. He saw the clothes and was filled with wonder. Jesus must be alive! Then he and Peter went back to their friends.

Mary had by now returned to the tomb, and she stood weeping outside it. She looked inside and saw two angels in the place where Jesus' body had been.

'Why are you crying?' they asked.

'Because they have taken away my Lord, and I don't know where he is,' she sobbed.

Then she turned and saw another figure standing behind her.

'Why are you crying? Who are you looking for?' he asked.

In the misty half light, and through her tears, Mary thought that this must be the gardener. So she said,

'Sir, if you have taken him away, tell me where you have taken him, and then I can go there.'

The figure said just one word, 'Mary!'

Mary knew that voice! No one else said 'Mary' like that! It was Jesus! Alive! She fell at his feet and cried,

'Master!'

'Do not touch me,' said Jesus, 'for I have not yet gone back to my Father. But go to my followers and tell them that I shall be returning to my Father, who is their Father, and to my God, who is their God too.'

Mary needed no second bidding. She ran back to the disciples who were still puzzled, and told them, 'I have *seen* the Lord!'

She told them all that Jesus had said.

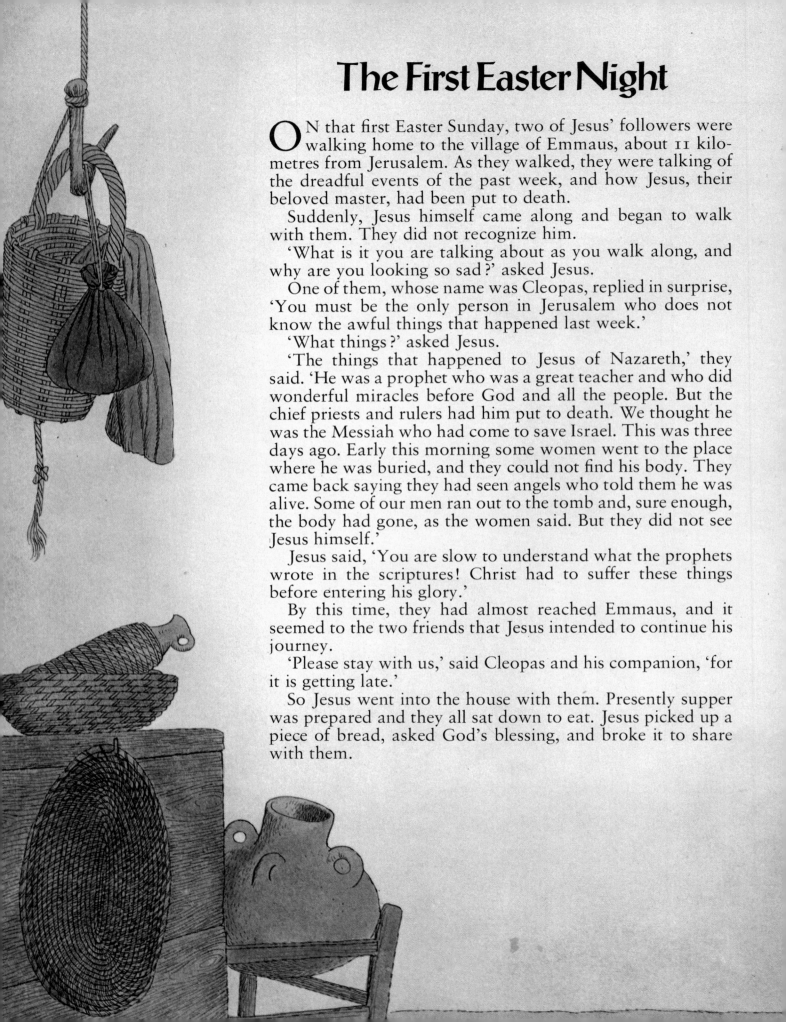

The First Easter Night

ON that first Easter Sunday, two of Jesus' followers were walking home to the village of Emmaus, about 11 kilometres from Jerusalem. As they walked, they were talking of the dreadful events of the past week, and how Jesus, their beloved master, had been put to death.

Suddenly, Jesus himself came along and began to walk with them. They did not recognize him.

'What is it you are talking about as you walk along, and why are you looking so sad?' asked Jesus.

One of them, whose name was Cleopas, replied in surprise, 'You must be the only person in Jerusalem who does not know the awful things that happened last week.'

'What things?' asked Jesus.

'The things that happened to Jesus of Nazareth,' they said. 'He was a prophet who was a great teacher and who did wonderful miracles before God and all the people. But the chief priests and rulers had him put to death. We thought he was the Messiah who had come to save Israel. This was three days ago. Early this morning some women went to the place where he was buried, and they could not find his body. They came back saying they had seen angels who told them he was alive. Some of our men ran out to the tomb and, sure enough, the body had gone, as the women said. But they did not see Jesus himself.'

Jesus said, 'You are slow to understand what the prophets wrote in the scriptures! Christ had to suffer these things before entering his glory.'

By this time, they had almost reached Emmaus, and it seemed to the two friends that Jesus intended to continue his journey.

'Please stay with us,' said Cleopas and his companion, 'for it is getting late.'

So Jesus went into the house with them. Presently supper was prepared and they all sat down to eat. Jesus picked up a piece of bread, asked God's blessing, and broke it to share with them.

Suddenly, they recognized him! They looked up in amazement – and he had vanished from their sight.

'We should have known,' they said to one another. 'Didn't it seem like a fire in our hearts while he was talking to us!'

Even though it was late, they were so excited that they immediately got up and hurried all the way back to Jerusalem.

There they told the disciples and other friends who were there of their wonderful experience!

As they were talking, Jesus himself suddenly appeared among them. They were frightened and thought they were seeing a ghost.

'Why are you so afraid?' asked Jesus. 'Look at my hands and my feet. Touch me and see.'

Jesus ate in front of them and talked to them, and slowly the disciples realized the wonderful truth that Jesus was still with them.

Breakfast on the Shore

'I'M going fishing,' said Peter one night to his disciple friends, James, John, Thomas, Nathanael and two others.

'We'll come with you,' they replied, and off they set in their boat into the darkness. As sometimes happened, it was a poor night for fishing and they caught nothing.

As they were returning at dawn they saw someone standing on the shore, but in the half light they could not see who it was.

'Have you caught anything?' the figure called out.

'Nothing at all,' they answered.

'Then throw your net over the right hand side of the boat and you will catch some,' said the man.

They did as the man said, and to their surprise, the net was so full of fish that they could not pull it in.

They were nearing the shore when John realized who the man was.

'It is the Lord!' he cried, and at once Peter jumped into the water and began to wade ashore. The others stayed to pull the loaded net on to the beach.

When they landed they saw a fire had been lit to cook the fish, and there was some bread.

'Bring some of the fish you've caught and we can have breakfast,' Jesus said.

Peter dragged in the net and counted the fish. There were one hundred and fifty three.

The Ascension

SOME time later, Jesus came again to his disciples as they were gathered on a hill in Galilee where he had told them to meet. Forty days had now passed since that first Easter Sunday when Jesus had risen from the dead. During those days he had appeared to them many times, and always he knew what had been happening and what they had been talking about before he came.

He had talked to them much about the kingdom of God, but they had not really understood. Some of them thought he was going to free Israel from Rome and make it the great nation it had once been.

Jesus told them their job was to go out and win the world for God. He knew they could not do this huge task if they relied on their own strength, so he said that they were not to leave Jerusalem until God's Spirit had come to help them.

'John baptized you with water,' he said, 'but you will be baptized with the Holy Spirit in a few days' time. Go and make disciples of all nations, baptizing them in the name of the Father, and of the Son, and of the Holy Spirit, and teaching them all I have told you. I will be with you always.'

As he spoke these words a cloud came and hid him from them and they saw him no more.

They were standing gazing at the sky and wondering, when two angels appeared before them.

'Men of Galilee,' they said, 'Why are you standing gazing up into heaven? Jesus has gone away to heaven, and some day he will come back again as you have seen him go.'

This was Jesus' last wonderful act on earth, and it is called his ascension.

The First Whitsunday

JERUSALEM was very busy and full of people. They were celebrating the feast of Pentecost, their harvest festival. People came from far and near, and many different languages could be heard in the city.

Pentecost (from a word meaning 'fifty') came fifty days after the Passover, which was the time Jesus had been crucified. However, his followers knew he had risen again, and it was now ten days since he had ascended into heaven.

The disciples and some other believers were gathered in a room in Jerusalem. They remembered that Jesus had told them not to leave Jerusalem until the Holy Spirit had come to them. They were waiting for this to happen because then they could begin their great task of winning the world for Christ.

All of a sudden, there was a great rushing sound, as though a mighty wind had sprung up, and it seemed to fill the whole house. Then what looked like tongues of flame appeared to settle over the heads of each one of them. This was God's sign that the Holy Spirit had come.

The effect on them was tremendous! They changed from being frightened, puzzled people, into people of great power and joy, who felt that nothing would stop them from going out to tell the world the truth about Jesus.

In some marvellous way, everyone who heard them speak, from whatever country they came, could understand what they said as though it was their own language.

'What is this?' the crowds exclaimed in amazement. 'Aren't these men from Galilee? Yet they can speak all our languages. We can all understand that they are telling us about the mighty works of God.'

Some of the crowd were scornful, and said the disciples had been drinking too much wine.

Peter stepped forward. He was not going to listen to talk like that! He stood with the other apostles and began to preach the first Christian sermon. He told them about Jesus' life and death. 'God has made him Lord and Messiah!' he said.

Many of the people listening were deeply moved at this, and some were very worried. They turned to Peter and the other apostles and asked, 'What should we do?'

Peter had no hesitation in replying, 'Repent of your sins and be baptized in the name of Jesus Christ. Your sins will be forgiven and you will receive the Holy Spirit. God's promise of the gift of his Holy Spirit is for everyone who will follow his way.'

Many people believed and came to be baptized, and about three thousand were added to the group of believers that day. They learnt from the apostles and joined in their prayers. Followers of Christ began to grow in number and they started to spread throughout the world.

Peter and John

THE first Christians brought the early Church into being. They shared all their belongings, and sold their fields, houses, and possessions, and gave the money to those in need. They met in the temple each day, and had their meals together in one another's homes. They went about, fearless of the authorities, praising God. Each day more and more people saw how happy true followers of Jesus are and they came to join them.

One afternoon Peter and John went to the temple at about three o'clock, which was the hour for prayer. They went through the gate which was called the Beautiful Gate, and sitting there was a man who had been lame all his life. He was over forty years old and every day he was carried to the gate to beg money from the people passing.

When he saw Peter and John, he held out his hand, hoping they would give him something. They looked straight at him, and Peter said, 'We haven't any money, but we will give you what we have. In the name of Jesus Christ of Nazareth, get up and walk!'

Peter took him by the right hand and helped him up, and the lame man felt the strength come into his feet and ankles. First he found he could stand on his feet, then he walked, and then he followed Peter and John into the temple, jumping for joy! He praised God who had given the power to Peter and John to heal him. The people who saw him walking were amazed, and they ran after Peter and John.

'Why are you staring at us?' asked Peter. 'It wasn't by our power that this man was made to walk. It was God's power and it was faith in Jesus that made him well.'

Then Peter began to tell them about Jesus and many of them believed.

While they were still talking, some priests and officials arrived. They were very annoyed that Peter and John dared to preach about Jesus, and they seized them and put them in jail.

The next day the high priest and other officials asked them, 'How did you do this? What power did you use?'

Peter told them it was the power of Jesus Christ.

The officials were amazed at this, for Peter and John seemed to be quite ordinary men. In the end the high priest let them go but he said they were not to teach or speak in the name of Jesus any more.

'Is it better to obey you or to obey God?' asked Peter. 'We are not able to keep quiet about Jesus and of all we have seen and heard.'

The officials warned them even more strongly, but they did not dare punish them because so many people were now on the side of Jesus and the apostles.

Stephen

THE number of people joining the Church continued to grow and the twelve apostles soon found they needed more people to help in the work. So they chose seven good men, one of whom was named Stephen. He performed many miracles among the people.

Some members of the synagogue did not like this, and they bribed a few men to say they had heard Stephen speaking against God. Although this was not true there were officials who believed it, and they arrested Stephen and took him before the council. More false witnesses were brought in.

The high priest asked Stephen, 'Is all this true?'

Stephen replied in a long speech. He told them how God had worked through Abraham, Joseph, Moses, David and Solomon, and that he had sent the prophets to tell people how to live in God's way.

'How stubborn you are!' said Stephen. 'You are just like your ancestors. You won't let the Holy Spirit live in your hearts. You are the ones who know God's law, and yet you refuse to obey it.'

The members of the council were furious at this. They covered up their ears with their hands so that they would not hear what they knew was the truth.

Stephen looked up to heaven and said, 'Look! I see the heavens are open and Jesus is at God's right hand.'

At this they all rushed at Stephen and threw him out of the city and stoned him to death.

As they stoned him, Stephen prayed. 'Lord Jesus,' he said, 'receive my spirit.'

Then he knelt down and, thinking of his persecutors, he prayed, 'Lord, do not remember the sins of these men.'

Having said this, Stephen died.

Peter and Cornelius

IN Caesarea there lived a captain in the Roman army named Cornelius. He was a kind man who helped the Jewish people, and he and his family worshipped God. One day he received a message from God, asking him to send some men to Joppa to bring back a man named Peter.

Peter did not know they were coming and he went up on to the roof of the house to pray.

Suddenly he had a strange vision. The heavens opened and something that looked like a great sheet came down, lowered by its four corners. In it were many kinds of animals, reptiles and birds. Then a voice said, 'Rise, Peter, kill and eat.'

'Certainly not!' said Peter. 'I have never eaten anything which we Jews consider unclean.'

The voice said, 'Do not call anything unclean which God says is clean.'

This happened three times and then the sheet went back to heaven. While Peter was wondering what it all meant, the three men sent by Cornelius arrived.

'Captain Cornelius wants you to come to his house, so that he can hear what you have to say,' they told Peter.

The next day, Peter and some of his Jewish friends from Joppa went to Caesarea with the men. There they found Cornelius waiting for them with his friends who were not Jews, but Gentiles.

Peter began to understand the meaning of his strange vision. He said to them,

'You all know that a Jew like me is not allowed to visit Gentiles like you. But God has shown me in a vision that I must not consider anyone unclean.' Then Peter told them he now realized that God's followers can be of any race and they are all equal in his eyes.

The Holy Spirit came to the Gentiles and they were baptized in the name of Jesus Christ.

Peter escapes from Prison

'INTO jail with him!' cried King Herod, and Peter was fastened with chains and put between two guards. Two more guards were posted at the prison gate, for Herod did not want his prisoners to escape. James, one of Jesus' followers had already been put to death by a sword, and Herod intended to persecute all Christians.

It was the time of the Passover, and Herod planned to have Peter put on trial as soon as the feast was over. While Peter lay in prison the members of the Church who were still free prayed to God for his safety.

The night before the trial, Peter was asleep, chained to his guards. Suddenly the cell was filled with a brilliant light. Peter awoke and looked up. He saw an angel standing in his cell! The angel shook him by the shoulder and said,

'Come on, Peter! Hurry and get up!'

To his great surprise, Peter's chains fell from his hands.

'Put on your sandals and your cloak, and come with me,' commanded the angel.

Peter thought he must be dreaming, but he got up and followed the angel out of prison. They passed the first guard post, and the second. The guards did not even try to seize Peter. 'This can't be real,' he thought.

When they came to the huge iron gate which led into the city, it swung open by itself and they found themselves in the street outside. Peter looked round and the angel had disappeared. He realized he had not been dreaming. He was free!

'Now I know that it was God who sent the angel to rescue me from Herod's clutches,' he said to himself. The guards would be chasing after him soon so he hurried to the house of John Mark's mother, Mary. He knocked, and a servant girl named Rhoda came to the door.

'Who is it?' she asked. She recognized Peter's voice when he answered and she was so excited and happy that she forgot to open the door! Instead she ran back to Mary, who was praying for Peter's safety with a number of friends.

'Peter's outside!' she exclaimed.

'You're mad!' they told her. 'He can't be. He's in jail!'

'No! No! It's true!' she insisted.

All this time, Peter went on knocking at the door. When at last someone came to open it, they found that it really was Peter.

Peter then came in, and asked them all to be quiet while he told them what had happened. They were so excited! Then he said he would go away and hide somewhere else for a while, for King Herod's soldiers were bound to search the houses of Peter's friends.

Next morning there was a great fuss at the prison. Where was Peter? Who had dared to let him escape? Why had the guards not done their job properly? Herod gave orders for a thorough search to be made, but though the soldiers hunted everywhere, they could not find Peter. When the search was finally given up, Herod questioned all the guards, and because he could get no satisfactory answers, he ordered them to be put to death.

The Conversion of Saul

AFTER Stephen was stoned, Jesus' followers in Jerusalem suffered dreadful persecution. One of the chief persecutors was a man named Saul. He was determined that this new group of believers should be destroyed at all costs.

Wherever he went he uttered murderous threats against the disciples of Jesus. How he hated them! From house to house he went, dragging out all the believers he could find and having them thrown into jail without good cause.

One day, Saul set out for Damascus, with several other men. They were determined to wipe out Jesus' followers there. They had nearly reached Damascus when suddenly, at about midday, there was a brilliant, blinding flash of light in the sky. It was so fierce that Saul fell to the ground, closing his eyes against its glare. Then he heard a voice say,

Saul! Saul! Why are you persecuting me?'

The men travelling with Saul were amazed and stood speechless, for they could hear the voice but could see no one speaking.

'Who are you?' asked Saul.

'I am Jesus, whom you are persecuting,' came the reply.

'What shall I do, Lord?' asked Saul, fearfully.

'Get up and go into the city, and there you will be told what you must do,' said the voice.

Saul struggled to his feet and opened his eyes – and found that he could not see. He could hear his friends around him, but could not see them. 'I am blind!' he gasped in horror.

His friends were bewildered. They took him by the hand and led him into Damascus. Three days went by and still Saul could not see. During that time he did not eat or drink.

Now in Damascus there was a man named Ananias who believed in God. Shortly after Saul and his companions arrived in the city, Ananias had a vision in which God said to him,

'Get ready and go to Straight Street, where a man named Saul from Tarsus is staying. He is praying and has had a vision. In his vision a man named Ananias comes to him and lays his hands on him so that he might see again.'

Ananias was not at all happy at being told to do this.

'But, Lord,' he protested, 'I've heard a lot about this man, and all the terrible things he has done to your followers in Jerusalem. Now he has come to Damascus, and I hear he has authority from the chief priests to arrest all the believers he finds.'

Then Ananias received a surprising reply. 'Go!' said God. 'This is the man I have chosen to serve me and to make my name known to all people.'

Ananias knew he must obey God's voice, even though it did not seem at all likely that Saul would become a believer. He went and did as he was told.

'Saul,' Ananias said to him, 'The Lord has sent me to you so that you might see again and be filled with the Holy Spirit. He has chosen you to be his witness to all men.'

Suddenly Saul could see again. He could see Ananias and the room where they were. He stood up and was baptized as a believer.

Then Saul had some food and his strength came back. Now he was ready to do anything God asked of him. By the power of the Holy Spirit he had become a changed man. He took on a new name, and from that time he was known as Paul. For the rest of his life he was one of God's great saints.

Paul's Shipwreck

PAUL went on three long and difficult journeys to other countries to tell people about Jesus. Nothing would stop him from trying to make new Christians in the many places he visited. When he had moved on he wrote letters to the Christians he had left behind to encourage them to be strong in their faith.

Paul had many enemies and he was often in danger of his life. He was also put in prison and stoned, but he still carried on with God's work.

On one occasion when he was in prison in Jerusalem, he appealed to the Emperor, which was his right as a Roman citizen. The governor, Festus, agreed to send him to Rome for trial before Caesar.

So Paul and his friend Luke, together with some other prisoners, were put on a ship bound for Rome.

They were coming close to Crete when a fierce storm blew up, driving the ship right off course. The men began to throw the cargo overboard to lighten the ship, but the waves continued to lash the ship, and they thought they would all drown. There were 276 people on board, and Paul said to them,

'Take courage! No one's life will be lost. We shall only lose the ship. Last night an angel of the God I worship told me this – and I trust in my God.'

The storm continued for two weeks and the ship was tossed about in the high seas. During this time, no one ate any food. At about midnight on the fourteenth night, the sailors suspected they were reaching land, and fearing that the ship would be dashed on the rocks, they lowered the anchors and prayed for daylight. Paul gave them some wise advice.

'You must all eat something,' he said and he set them an example by taking a piece of bread and thanking God. Everyone soon cheered up and began to eat.

When daylight came, they found they were in a bay, and as they tried to run the ship aground it hit a sandbank. The bows got stuck and the stern was soon shattered by the force of the waves.

'We'd better kill all the prisoners in case they swim ashore and escape,' decided the soldiers on board; but the officer in charge would not allow this. He wanted particularly to save Paul.

'No,' he said. 'Everyone who can swim must jump overboard and head for the shore. The rest can follow, holding on to planks or other broken pieces of the ship.'

In this way they all got safely ashore and, as Paul had said, no lives were lost.

They soon discovered that they were on the island of Malta. The natives were friendly and made them welcome. As it had started to rain and was cold, they made a fire, and Paul helped by gathering sticks. He was just putting them on the fire when a snake crawled out and fastened itself to his hand. The natives looked on with horror.

'This man must be a murderer,' they said. 'He has escaped the sea, but justice has sent the snake to kill him.'

Paul shook off the snake into the fire. When the natives realized he was unharmed, they changed their minds and said he was a god.

The ruler of the island was called Publius and he made Paul and the others welcome as his guests. It happened that his father was very ill, and when Paul heard this, he went to see him. He prayed for God's help, put his hands on the old man, and by the power of the Holy Spirit, he healed him. As soon as this news got about, many other sick people on the island came to be healed.

After three months Paul and the others from the ship were able to sail away, and the natives of Malta gave them many useful things for the voyage.

At last they arrived in Rome, and Paul was allowed to live in a house, provided there were soldiers to guard him all the time. He saw many people and told them about Jesus. From morning to night he worked hard explaining God's message to everyone he met, and writing to those whom he was unable to meet.

After two years he was brought before the Emperor who gave orders to execute him. Paul gave his life for Jesus.

The Armour of God

WHEN Paul was in prison, he was able to look closely at the soldiers who were set to guard him.

The special armour which they wore reminded him of the armour which every Christian needs to protect himself from evil. Christians must fight a constant battle against the forces of evil, and for this they need to be properly equipped.

The soldier wore a fairly loose tunic, and the first thing he put on when he went on duty was his *belt*. The belt is like truth, thought Paul, and you must buckle on the belt of Jesus' truth tightly so that there is no room for evil.

Next came the big curved *breastplate* to protect the soldier from sword-thrusts and arrows. If you live according to God's laws it helps to protect you from evil.

The soldier's *shoes* reminded Paul of eagerness to spread the word of God. Knowing the word of God gives you a firm foothold in life and makes you want to tell others about him.

Next came the soldier's huge *shield*. This, Paul felt, was like faith. A firm faith in God will protect you against all kinds of troubles.

Then the soldier put on his *helmet* to protect his head. This was like salvation which means being saved from sin by Jesus. You need God's help to overcome temptations.

Lastly, there was the soldier's *sword*. The Christian's sword is God's word. The word is in the Bible and in the ways God speaks to you in your daily life.

'Put on the armour of God,' Paul wrote in one of his letters, 'and you will be able to stand firm against evil.'